Cycle Time Management

The Fast Track to Time-Based Productivity Improvement

Cycle Time Management®

The Fast Track to Time-Based Productivity Improvement

Patrick Northey
Nigel Southway

Foreword by Brian A. Bennett
Publisher's Message by Norman Bodek

Productivity Press

Cambridge, Massachusetts   Norwalk, Connecticut

Productivity Press
P.O. Box 3007
Cambridge, Massachusetts 02140
United States of America
Telephone: (6l7) 497-5146
Telefax: (617) 868-3524

Cover design by Gary Ragaglia
Printed and bound by BookCrafters
Printed in the United States of America on acid-free paper

Library of Congress Cataloging-in-Publication Data

Northey, Patrick.
   Cycle time management: the fast track to time-based productivity improvement/Patrick Northey, Nigel Southway; foreword by Brian A. Bennett; publisher's message by Norman Bodek.
       p.   cm.
   Includes bibliographical references and index.
   ISBN 1-56327-015-3
   1. Product life cycle. 2. Product management. 3. Competition. 4. Time management. I. Southway, Nigel. II. Title.
HF5415.155.N67   1993
658.5'15—dc20   92-32449
                                                                            CIP

93 94 95 10 9 8 7 6 5 4 3 2 1

Contents

Publisher's Message

The priority economic issue in North America in the next decade is cycle time as the catalyst for improved productivity. *Cycle Time Management: The Fast Track to Time-Based Productivity Improvement* describes a change process that grounds an organization in cycle time improvement methods. Cycle time theory is the window through which you must look to analyze and drive your organization and its activities to maximum productivity. This book is an implementation guide that details the steps of a fast-track changeover to Cycle Time Management (CTM). From two Canadian authors and their firms, whose aggressive methods allow companies to change rapidly to time-based management throughout an organization, this fast-track process trains all the people in the organization to execute the CTM implementation themselves. With this approach, CTM becomes not just a change of strategy and method, but a powerful event that unifies an organization and allows it to sustain change over the long term.

In CTM, the processes of the entire organization are linked, from a CEO's strategic direction to the breakeven point in sales of the new product that implements that strategy. If such linkages are to work smoothly, the whole organization must become structured around time-based operational strategies. The role of CEOs and top managers, therefore, will be to manage cycle time. They will be required to collapse processes to the minimum essentials; to articulate strategic direction and company performance in terms of time related to market demand; and to establish an accounting infrastructure based on time. To do this requires a cultural and structural shift that ordinarily would take years to accomplish. The authors here, however, provide the means to achieve this organizational shift to cycle time management rapidly and with resounding success. Cases of actual implementation and its benefits are cited, and a description of the twelve-step implementation process is given. Pitfalls in establishing the cycle time approach are discussed with methods for overcoming resistance and difficulties that naturally arise in the midst of such a change process. The authors also present the necessity of achieving activity-based costing (ABC) to support cycle time management with a description of ABC's method and benefits.

Patrick Northey, president of Interaction, Inc., an Ontario consulting firm and coauthor with Nigel Southway of *Cycle Time Management,* has stated that two elements are critical to sustained, successful continuous improvement environments: a single performance measure that encourages the integration of all employees into one organizational team, and a process that enables the CEO to manage the change in a controlled way. Time as the measure of productivity satisfies both and provides a generic framework that is applicable to any work environment: in hospitals, it is Length of Stay (LOS), in manufacturing and service processes, it is Cycle Time. This shift to cycle time management causes an emergence of a new cost model (ABC) in organizations; it simplifies internal controls and improves profits overall. However, to implement it you have to be able to ask *why* about everything you are doing, every step of the way, from concept to product delivery in manufacturing, from admission of patients to their release in hospitals, from initial account opening to the development of full service for clients in a financial institution. In each organizational setting, unnecessary steps and delays must be eliminated until only essential activities remain.

In the early 1900s, Frederick Taylor's time and motion studies, and more recently in the 1970s and 1980s, Shigeo Shingo's revolutionary methods of eliminating waste in production processes, laid the foundation for a shift to time-based management. Shingo's work in quick changeover methods (*A Revolution in Manufacturing: The SMED System*, Cambridge, MA: Productivity Press, 1983) led to the elimination of inventories (stockless production) and the possibility of high diversity, small-lot production. In the nineties the focus of waste elimination practices has turned to the front end of manufacturing — product development. Shingo's methods and those of his successors have been modified to reduce time and errors in designing new products. Kenichi Sekine has adapted the methods of one-piece flow and U-shaped cells to the design process (*Cutting Design Times in Half*, Cambridge, MA: Productivity Press, 1993). Methods from the TQM methodology such as concurrent engineering, quality function deployment, and hoshin kanri reduce breakdown time while eliminating errors and expenses that are usually not recognized until production. Methods such as hoshin kanri or concurrent engineering, which enforce an internal communication system early in the strategic and product design stages, are the most recent evolution of the quality movement in organizations.

Cycle time management provides a structure within which such methods may succeed, where time becomes the unifying factor for implementing strategy, communicating between departments, defining goals, and measuring performance. Cycle time management is a generic process, applicable to banks, hospitals, service business, and of course manufacturing. This fast track to CTM applies a process for doing business in a hierarchical structure and bureaucracy and leads the way to a complete realization of a continuous improvement environment. We encourage managers interested in achieving lasting competitive positions to embrace the approach described in this book.

We at Productivity Press would like to thank the authors, Patrick Northey and Nigel Southway, for the right to publish their book, as well as the Ontario consulting firm Cycle Time Management, Inc., which created this fast-track method for changing organizations to the time-based approach. We express our thanks also to those who participated in creating this book in its final form: Dorothy Lohmann and Laura St. Clair for editorial services, David Lennon, Karla Tolbert, Gayle Joyce, and Caroline Kutil for composition and production, and Gary Ragaglia for the cover design.

Norman Bodek, President
Diane Asay, Series Editor

Foreword

Most managers within a business environment know what needs to be done in order to compete successfully today.

Most just don't know where to start. They've read all the books, heard all the buzz words, and have been told countless times how good the Japanese are until they're sick and tired of hearing it.

This book sets out to rectify that feeling of the rabbit frozen in the headlights by using cycle time reduction as the driver and focus for improvements in *all* facets of a business.

Don't be afraid to get started; don't be afraid to make mistakes (and you will); most mistakes can be corrected once the forward momentum begins.

It may require a leap of faith — especially by the accountants; and more than a few paradigm shifts, as it did in our Tennessee operation where much credit goes to the vice president of manufacturing. Unionized or non-unionized, you can be sure that the guys on the floor want to do a good job, want to produce good quality and want to partipate — all you have to do is provide the vehicle and the climate for them to do it.

The CTM process is such a vehicle. It is the "how to." It provides the structure, the discipline, the education, and the facilitation needed to get you there. It's a long journey and it isn't easy, but it can be done. The CTM process is a total-participation, people program, and not a gee-whiz, hi-tech, capital-intensive, bells-and-whistles program. First you install the process — and then you can add the other programs later.

The CTM process becomes a way of life, a way of doing business that can reach every corner of the operation. When everyone embraces it, it can deliver significant results. For example, under our focused factory strategy the CTM techniques were instructional in achieving major productivity gains in our factories and were crucial in the smooth assimilation of a newly acquired $200 million, 550,000 square foot, 700-person operation. The CTM process gave us a solid foundation, confidence, and training to make and handle the necessary changes.

Strategically, we have to be much closer to our customers. We must know and respond to their needs much faster, deliver an even wider choice of high-quality products and continually do it better. And, at the same time we have to provide a solid return on assets. Already, CTM has played an important role for us, and we have not yet applied it to such areas as supply management and distribution.

Make a start. Go for it. Those who don't may not exist beyond the year 2000. To borrow from Mark Twain: "If you think education is expensive — try ignorance."

Brian Bennett
Senior Vice President
Inter-City Products Corporation (USA)

Acknowledgments

Although the words and concepts in this book are the authors' responsibility, we wish to thank several people for their interest and ideas.

We thank William Neeve and Uri Wittenberg of Cycle Time Management, Inc. for their knowledge and expertise in manufacturing and time-based strategies, and their assistance, as well as their willingness to let us use the CTM graphics and education material. We also thank Karen Neeve for developing many of the graphics, and Maureen Tuohy for developing others as well as assembling the final graphics.

Thanks also to Don Kivell and Kit Staley for providing the KeepRite statistics and for allowing us to interview key employees.

We are grateful to Brian Bennett for the foreword, and to Brian Walton, who conducted the interviews that are so important to the KeepRite case.

Finally, we thank Diane Asay for her forbearance and helpful editing advice.

A special thanks from Patrick Northey

I would like to thank Ian Ross, Bob Nielson, Gary Corlette, and Fred Hedley, all of whom provided useful insights in their special fields.

I am also indebted to my wife, Margot, and Pam Young for their patience and considerable editing and writing skills during the writing period. Brenda Northey deserves thanks for retyping several chapters that unfortunately were erased at a critical point in the process.

A special thanks from Nigel Southway

Writing a book about a subject that we as authors hold close to our hearts can be disruptive to the peace and stability of past and present relationships with colleagues, friends, family, and loved ones.

Thanks to everyone for your contribution, understanding, and commitment. Maybe the next book won't be so hard . . . maybe!

I especially dedicate this book to my absent friends Keith Boulter, Pete York, and Brian Price, who early in my life helped me understand the power of teamwork and commitment;

To my parents, who had no idea that I would co-write a book;

To my many colleagues in corporations who provided encouragement and inspiration in developing what eventually became the CTM 12-step implementation process;

To the CTM, Inc. team, for creating the time and encouragement to write this book.

And especially to Sheila, without whose support my contribution to this book could not have been made.

Introduction

This book outlines a strategic management process called Cycle Time Management (CTM). It shows how you can use CTM to reduce cycle time in your company — dramatically increasing productivity and profits.

These days global competitiveness is forcing companies of all sizes to go to ever-greater lengths to improve customer satisfaction. If companies continue to use traditional operating practices, they will be unable to meet these new demands. However, if they focus on cycle time as their productivity measure, they can both decrease delivery time and improve quality, obviously creating a more satisfied customer.

A company's total business cycle time is measured from the time a customer's need is identified to receipt of payment from that customer for the finished product. The best analogy is a relay race. The time begins with the starting gun and ends when the last runner breaks the tape at the finish line. It includes all the time required to run each leg, as well as the time required to transfer the baton at the end of each leg. Total business cycle time includes any or all of the following subcycles or loops:

- *The make/ship loop.* The time from receipt of material, through the value-adding conversion steps, to shipment or transfer of a finished product to the distribution loop.
- *The distribution loop.* The time from finished production to shipment to the customer from the distribution warehouse.
- *The supply loop.* The time from release of the purchase order to receipt of the correct materials in the right quantities at the right point in the manufacturing process.

- *The new product introduction (NPI) loop.* The time from identification of the need for a new product to delivery of the first unit of product to a customer.
- *The strategic business development loop.* The time required to develop a new strategy, make the decision to adopt it, and then implement it.

In the last decade, it has become clear that the compartmentalization of these loops has inhibited competitiveness. This book demonstrates why all the loops must be integrated if total business cycle time is to be reduced. But let's first examine each loop in more detail.

THE MAKE/SHIP LOOP

In the 1980s most companies trying to make improvements focused on this loop. Prior to 1980, a long backlog of orders in this loop created a sense of complacency. This complacency rippled through the distribution and supply loops also. As long as customers tolerated the long wait, the system worked, because it enabled the manufacturing process to "minimize product cost" by using "economical" batch sizes. This approach increased the total cycle time, but time was not perceived as a critical issue.

When customers started demanding shorter delivery times and were able to get them from competitors, a problem arose. Sales departments responded to this competition in the following ways:

- They persuaded manufacturing to commit to unrealistic delivery times. As a result, sales departments soon discovered that they were constantly having to break promises to customers; to keep all customers happy, they had to become internal expeditors, which increased the tension with manufacturing.
- They increased factory orders for finished goods and distribution inventory. This increase put even more pressure on manufacturing, and the ensuing loss of trust led to second-guessing between marketing and manufacturing. In addition, the already uncertain sales forecast used to order material supplies had to be

made even further in advance, since the suppliers were caught in the same time squeeze. As the forecast period was extended, the potential for error and disagreement increased.

A double problem arose for those organizations whose competitors *could* deliver the correct product in a measurably shorter cycle time. The lower cycle time meant that these competitors could produce at lower cost and did not require such large inventories, which further reduced their costs. Not only were the slower companies struggling to compete, but they were faced with margin problems due to the higher costs of inventory and waste in the structure.

The reaction of some manufacturers was to reduce their inventories. The first industries to take this "cold shower" tack were electronics and computers. The automotive, shipbuilding, and quality commodity goods industries jumped in soon after. For a while the "slimming pill" worked. But as competitors with shorter cycle times continued to steal market share, it became obvious that to survive, companies would have to do things differently, not just do them harder.

The Focus Shifts to Time

The next villain manufacturers focused on was the excessive time required by the manufacturing cycle. To reduce cycle time, many companies initially relied on new technology. Although technology has a role in the new cycle time-focused approach, it is an expensive and often ineffective way to start. One aim of this book is to encourage companies to simplify their existing processes — to eliminate waste or nonessential activities. The reality is that as many as 90 percent of the existing activities are nonessential and can be eliminated. The benefit of focusing on internal processes is that the changes are relatively inexpensive and the operating savings relatively large. Furthermore, it usually creates a one-time working capital reduction. This frees up credit or cash and will help to release the resources required to further reduce cycle time, purchase new technology, reduce loans, or fund new research and development.

As soon as manufacturers focused on processes, they could see the waste associated with changeovers, quality defects, process control, factory layout, machine downtime, and scheduling. They soon realized they could dramatically reduce the make/ship loop cycle time.

As the manufacturing cycle time started to decrease, it became apparent that the cycle time for processing a customer's purchase order was greater than the time it took to manufacture the product. This was not surprising because in the traditional environment of long manufacturing cycle time, there is no incentive to rush the customer order paperwork through. It will only sit in the queue until manufacturing is ready for it.

An example from one client company, a manufacturer of printed circuit boards, illustrates the point. The customer expectation for delivery time was running at 35 days — exactly what the company quoted as their delivery time. However, when the time it took for the average sales order to go through order entry was measured, it was found to be a mere 10 days. The true processing time was actually only 20 minutes.

While reducing the cycle time in the make/ship loop is the logical place to start, reducing this loop's cycle time in isolation will not be enough to satisfy customer demands for better quality products, delivered more quickly. Once you reduce cycle time in the make/ship loop, the activities in the other traditional loops become the next focus for improvement. Moreover, the internal pressure to reduce inventory costs will force companies to focus on reducing cycle time in their distribution systems.

THE DISTRIBUTION LOOP

The complexities associated with the distribution loop vary from business to business. Some organizations have complex distribution networks; others have simple ones. In all companies, however, the customer order starts the process.

The order may go through a distributor or directly to the company. The issue is not how many hands the order goes through, but what essential role these hands play in the process and how long the process takes. For example, distributors may not be providing timely sales information because they are using the order-point method of signaling their needs. This can delay arrival of the information to the manufacturing process for several days. Some companies have taken advantage of computer networking systems to provide sales order information on a daily basis.

There are significant benefits to reducing cycle time in distribution systems. A 50 percent reduction in distribution cycle time is not unattainable. The resulting simplified process enables staff to reduce inventories, improve the quality of service, and reduce general sales order expenses and associated supporting labor costs.

A dramatic example of shortening the distribution cycle time is now affecting the eyeglass retail industry. By locating the lens grinding facilities right in their stores, the retailers can now reduce their total business cycle time to "about an hour," as the commercial says. They have no inventories to track, negligible administration costs, and a better shot at guaranteed customer satisfaction. In addition, they can capitalize on this phenomenal cycle time advantage in their advertising.

THE SUPPLY LOOP

Although the supply loop is a significant contributor to the total business cycle time, most companies are powerless to force suppliers to reduce their cycle times. Only large companies, such as the automotive giants, have had enough clout to insist that their material be delivered "just-in-time." Even with them, most suppliers did not take the necessary measures to reduce their own cycle time.

For most suppliers, "business as usual" means that they keep a fully stocked warehouse to feed the daily demand and pass on the added cost. This bizarre version of JIT simply increases the supplier's cost of doing business.

Until suppliers develop their own programs for reducing internal cycle time, the objective for most companies will be to ensure the stability of material deliveries by encouraging the supplier's efforts to improve quality. Reliable sources of material will enable both supplier and customer to predict safety stock levels more accurately and therefore will reduce the risk of shutting down the main line.

Unfortunately, this approach has proved effective only for standard-use raw materials and components for which there is an unchanging demand. For custom-made outsourced parts with long lead times, manufacturing has had to rely mainly on the accuracy of the sales forecast. The longer the forecast, the greater the potential for error.

By contrast, reducing the supply cycle time pays off, because it reduces the length of the forecast and therefore improves its accuracy. As well, the supplier, if in partnership with the customer, can better develop its own raw material forecast, decreasing the potential for error.

THE NEW PRODUCT INTRODUCTION LOOP

In most markets and industries the temperature is definitely rising. Staying competitive with yesterday's products will be difficult, if not impossible. However, being first or best with a new product in the 1990s may mean developing a new product in *weeks,* not years. To succeed, therefore, many corporations will have to dramatically reduce their new product introduction (NPI) time while continuing to consistently and profitably meet customer expectations about price, quality, and function.

As product life cycles continue to decrease, the key to success will be to integrate (1) new product strategies, (2) new product research, (3) product development, and (4) launch activities — into one effective short-cycle capability that can respond consistently to ever-increasing market demands.

The successful organizations in the 1990s will be structured either formally or informally into multifunctional product teams with market segmentation by product to aggressively attack these new product and market opportunities. The product-team approach fits right into the CTM concept of the team approach and amplifies the concept of multifunctional harmony.

To minimize the new product introduction cycle time requires an organization that has already minimized cycle times in the other loops and is able to integrate them with this loop.

THE STRATEGIC BUSINESS DEVELOPMENT LOOP

The strategic business development loop is probably the most poorly managed of all loops. This is not because the people involved lack skill or intelligence, but because they do not fully understand the high financial returns to be gained from improving this loop's cycle time.

This loop, as defined earlier, is where the company's strategic planning platform unfolds. In it are answered the questions, how do we grow, acquire, integrate, and develop the company?

Many books and articles have been written on the correct way to manage this loop, some even hint on how to improve the cycle time. Few (if any) expose this loop as the prime mover for total business improvement. Fancy words such as *synergy* and *market share* and *capital contribution* are used. Rarely, however, is the overall business cycle time labeled as either an area for improvement or a parameter to be coordinated through the strategic business development process.

Let us consider the four main thrusts in this loop, which are to grow, acquire, integrate, and develop. We should also consider the reverse strategies: shrink, divest, separate, and liquidate. All organizations have undertaken at least one of these eight strategies. If any could be done faster both the corporation and the customer would benefit. Too often, however, this loop is encumbered by size, politics, economics, and legal and financial inertia. The corporations that can eliminate red tape, and minimize the time required to make and execute decisions will be able to survive in the 1990s. Those that cannot meet those demands will not make it into the next century.

Unfortunately, many companies have not even started to reduce their total business cycle times. The result is that not only are they denied short new product development and strategic planning cycle times, but they are failing to meet rising customer expectations for shorter delivery times, higher quality, and wider product variety. The only way to keep up is to integrate the supply, make/ship, and distribution loops into one short–cycle-time manufacturing loop.

The advantages of one short–cycle-time business loop are clear:

- It is flexible.
- It enables the company to respond promptly to customer requests.
- It ensures quick delivery of high-quality, low-cost products.

In other words, managing businesses by cycle time will be essential in the future. As George Stalk states bluntly, time is the next source of competitive advantage.[1]

HOW CTM BENEFITS THE WHOLE ORGANIZATION

A time-driven approach brings order to the productivity improvement process. Instead of being overwhelmed by a large number of seemingly disjointed projects, you can integrate projects at a higher level and implement changes in a systematic way. Time becomes the overall productivity measure.

Cycle Time Management yields benefits that extend beyond manufacturing into marketing, human resources, and finance. For example, once service personnel learn that as much as 90 percent of the activities in their work area are nonessential and expendable, they become open to a new operating strategy.

Sales people, too, see major benefits from reducing cycle time, because such a measure shortens customer response time, while continuously improving quality. As well, they like the resulting lower inventory levels and costs, and greater flexibility in price negotiations.

Human resources staff appreciate the companywide involvement necessitated by programs to reduce cycle time. They know that it is easier to build a team if there is one common goal (cycle time reduction) and one productivity measure (cycle time). They also like the Cycle Time Management implementation framework because it provides an orderly process for integrating everybody into a team to reduce cycle time.

Finally, Cycle Time Management encourages managers to use a more participative style while controlling the pace of change. If you are still skeptical, consider these cases:

- A Canadian Motorola division reduced its cycle time from 35 days to 5 days.
- A Blount Canada plant in Guelph, Ontario, which makes prolite bars for chain saws, cut its cycle time from 21 days to 1 day.[2]
- In Cincinnati, a General Electric plant that services turbine blades reduced its cycle time from 13 weeks to 1-to-3 days.[3]

It is certainly possible to eliminate waste without instituting CTM practices; many companies have already demonstrated this. More at issue are *how fast* you can reduce cycle time and *how well* you can keep control of a number of disparate projects. Many managers have told us that it was the fear of losing control that led them to opt for a piecemeal, project-oriented approach to cycle time reduction rather than commit to an aggressive, companywide cycle time reduction process — what we call the CTM fast-track approach. Cycle Time Management eliminates the uncertainty by providing an orderly way to move from the old culture to the new practices.

In short, because it focuses on time, CTM helps companies produce products of better quality at lower cost and with quicker delivery. These results are essential if companies are going to respond to increased global competition. The fast-track implementation method described here offers managers means of achieving these results in the shortest time and the most controlled and orderly way possible.

NOTES

1. George Stalk, "Time — The Next Source of Competitive Advantage," *Harvard Business Review*, July-August 1988, p. 41
2. Richard J. Schonberger, *World Class Manufacturing: The Lessons of Simplicity Applied* (New York: The Free Press, 1986), p. 231.
3. Ibid.

1
Fast-Track
Cycle Time Reduction:
The ICP KeepRite Case

The KeepRite story is more than a record of dramatic productivity improvement. It is also the tale of an extraordinary culture change within the workplace. It describes how employees from all levels learned to work as a team. The Evolution Plan was accepted by the Approval Team in October 1989. From that time to March 1991, the teams reduced company cycle time from 22 days to 7 and slashed inventories from $18 million to $3 million.

COMPANY BACKGROUND

Founded in 1948 with a commitment to build the very best air-conditioning products, KeepRite has consistently met the industry challenge for quality and reliability. It is the undisputed industry leader in Canada. Today as part of Inter-City Products, KeepRite Canada manufactures a complete range of air-conditioning products for residential and light commercial applications, as well as a comprehensive line of gas, oil, and electric-fired furnaces, space heaters, and unit heaters.

The total yearly sales, both domestic and foreign, has grown from $1 million in 1948 to about $200 million in 1989. KeepRite executives feel they have achieved this growth by adhering closely to the company's original philosophy, to build better-quality products through solid engineering and to back them up with technical competence and good service.

A TRADITIONAL BATCH PLANT

"Keep the lines operating at any cost," used to be the main objective of plant manager Don Kivell. Each machine — in fact, each department — was a discrete unit that was scheduled separately and measured independently. Listen to how lead hand and union steward Ron Sakardi describes the old production practices: "Setups were too long — I'd do a job for an hour and then had to do a two- or three-hour setup. Quality was bad. There was inventory all over the place and the plant wasn't safe. Looked like we were producing more scrap than production, but employees didn't give a damn."

As production manager and 20-year veteran Roy Winger recalls, "Line stoppages and parts shortages were common. We had three or four warehouses to cope with excessive inventories. While we scrambled for parts, people would be sent home for two to three days because we couldn't run product for the eight hours. We had no time for quality. We had lost control. Everyone was pretty defensive." The union was upset because one of the unique features of this plant was an elaborate piecework compensation scheme that had been an integral part of the culture for many years. Consequently, many members' wages were dramatically affected when they were sent home.

Control was not easy to recover. Kit Staley, the eventual CTM coordinator, explains that "the organization had no way of controlling the flow or costings because the MRP was out of control. Inventory accuracy was 35 percent to 40 percent. Bill-of-material accuracy was 15 percent to 20 percent. As a result, I used to spend two to three hours each morning in meetings discussing data inaccuracies."

The impact of the poor computer system was far more pervasive. Penny Pickering in Materials Planning recalls that "people didn't trust the computer; consequently, they did things manually." These parallel information systems inevitably led to a situation in which "office and plant personnel didn't talk to each other, or if they did, no one was really listening. There was a lot of frustration — everyone was doing their own thing."

Against that backdrop of confusion, frustration, and distrust, one group had created excitement by their actions in the paint shop. The "Linebackers" team had identified the outdated paint booth as a bottleneck and then designed a new booth and had it built by an outside company. The cost of the booth was $280,000. The overall savings, however, was significantly greater: $480,000 per year and a reduction of changeover time to 10 minutes. The Linebackers won a quality award with the project.

This project would later be cited as evidence of what teams could accomplish. In spite of its success, however, people remained skeptical about the depth of senior management's commitment to change.

MANAGEMENT PHILOSOPHY

It was at this point that senior managers called for help — outside help. They realized that to become a world-class organization, they would have to abandon traditional *batch* processing and move toward linear-flow *pull* manufacturing, which their Japanese competitors were using. While they would have to initiate the change process and provide constant support themselves, they would need outside facilitation skills to guide the evolution. They also concluded that the fastest way to get the company through such a major "culture shock" was to involve all their people. Consequently, they chose a change process in which they, as well as all their employees, would have to participate and be trained. In doing so they made a strong commitment to

- understanding new manufacturing techniques such as cycle time and linear pull systems
- investing in similar workshops for all employees
- involving all levels of personnel in planning
- implementing the changes required to reduce cycle time dramatically
- allowing people enough time to understand the process
- a participative management style, which meant giving up their roles as autocrats to become facilitators and coaches

The objective throughout the process was to reduce overall cycle time — from receipt of customer order to delivery of and payment for the product.

SUMMARY OF THE EVOLUTION PROCESS

The first step was to get all managers who were on either the approval team or the planning forum trained in the new operating techniques. The approval team, which consisted of senior managers, was expected to assign the resources on the basis of recommendations from the planning forum. The planning forum participants were middle managers and key employees whose job was to prepare the evolution plan — the framework by which to manage the transition to CTM.

As soon as the management training session ended, the planning forum established 15 review teams of middle managers and key employees. Those who needed it were trained quickly. All teams were then brought together, given their mandates, and sent off in search of opportunities to reduce cycle time.

The objective of each training session was to give everyone an understanding of the new concepts. There were other benefits too. At the first coffee break of the management session some observed that this was the first time that senior managers and all operating department heads had sat down in one room to discuss the business. Some senior managers suggested afterward that the improved communications alone would more than justify the training session's cost.

Yet while communication between all levels improved, only a few managers were initially willing to make a commitment to change. Most adopted a wait-and-see stance. Penny Pickering describes the middle managers' attitude best: "People were interested but skeptical at first. They were watching to see if the executives meant it." However, each director knew, as Kit Staley points out, that "Brian Bennett, the V.P. of manufacturing, was totally committed from the start."

Employees on the shop floor had mixed feelings. As Ron Sakardi explains: "They wanted to help themselves but not the company." However, most workers' information was sketchy since only the union representatives had any training. Don Kivell sensed the concern on the floor. He took advantage of the waiting period to "build trust and credibility" by staging many informal meetings with supervisory and shop-floor employees and committing resources to cleaning up the bill of material, resolving some of the safety issues, and establishing good housekeeping practices. His actions sparked interest.

This was a trying period because nothing appeared to be happening. Some of the most creative in the rank and file grew impatient because they were still not involved in the process. After three months, however, the evolution plan was ready to be presented to the approval team.

Impact of the Approval Team Meeting

The approval team meeting, which lasted for a full day, turned out to be the most important meeting in KeepRite's history. All 120 people involved with the 15 review teams were present; each team made presentations. In all, the evolution plan comprised 120 cycle time reduction projects ranked according to team priorities.

The meeting exceeded everyone's expectations. As John Chambers, manager of quality assurance, puts it, "Everyone burst into flower." Kit Staley remembers that "approval team members were blown away by the caliber of the presentations." They were also startled that most of the projects needed to reduce cycle time significantly would require little money and could be completed quickly. Furthermore, the initial skepticism of both senior managers and other employees gave way to enthusiasm. Management no longer doubted that employees were capable of working in teams to plan and implement improvements. Similarly, employees were convinced that senior managers were totally committed to reducing cycle time.

Action Teams

Action teams were organized within two weeks and then trained. Where needed, special training was provided in areas such as pull systems, project planning, preventive maintenance, blueprint reading, and team building.

Working On the First Projects

After the approval team meeting, the base of employee participation was moved down to operators and clerical staff. As Don Kivell puts it, "Credibility was cemented when people at the bottom were asked to become involved with teams and contribute their ideas. There were more volunteers than teams. A couple of teams got quick success, and we found lots of ways to celebrate those successes."

As an example, Ron Sakardi grabbed the chance to eliminate a major safety hazard — the degreaser. By eliminating the degreaser, Ron and some of his colleagues stopped the deterioration to the roof and reduced maintenance and repair of boilers. Furthermore, as a result of an operator's suggestion, they installed a bank of fans under the conveyor system and thus were able to reduce the new degreasing process from three days to 20 minutes. To those involved, the project indicated that management was serious about reducing cycle time.

Kit Staley reports on the overall success of the projects: "Results achieved were way beyond expectations. We had planned over five years, but in every area immediate dramatic improvement was evident."

A NEW SPIRIT OF TRUST

At the same time that project teams were starting on their projects, the company realized that they would have to slash production in response to a changed market. The result was a dramatic layoff of about 40 percent of shop-floor personnel. Normally, this kind of catastrophe would have killed enthusiasm. Yet because people had a new trust in management and faith in the company, the momentum remained and morale stayed positive.

Roy Winger was impressed that "we became less defensive and supervisors got together on problems in a common bond and stopped trying to point fingers." John Chambers adds, "People have started to look, question, and talk about things in a cooperative way." For Penny Pickering, the projects produced an "excitement in the air. People were talking about their presentations and ideas."

Even union-management relations had improved. As Ron Sakardi notes, "The company understands us better and we understand them."

Between October 1989 (when the approval team accepted the Evolution Plan) and March 1991, employees had produced the results shown in Table 1-1.

KeepRite Accomplishments	Baseline October 1989	March 1991
Reductions		
Overall cycle time	22 days	7 days
Inventory	$18 million	$3 million
WIP	12%	6%
Storage space	150,000 square feet	30,000 square feet
Order entry time	7 days	18 hours
Setup to presses	5 days	54 minutes
Work orders to presses	6 days	10 hours
Processing to presses	3 days	4 hours
Forklifts	28 trucks	16 trucks
Downtime	1200 hours	600 hours
Improvement (%)		
Inventory accuracy	50%	95%
Productivity core & header	100 hours	47 hours
Redraw drawings	207 drawings	21 drawings
Baseline Cycle Time		
Starting point is August 1988		
Productivity improvement	up 17%	
Operating profits	up 219%	
Delivery schedule	96% on-time delivery	
Shipments	up 29%	
Overtime	50% below budget	
Inventory	25% ($5 million) below budget	

Table 1-1. Results of Cycle Time Reduction at KeepRite

EPILOGUE

Two years after producing such successful results, Roy Winger observes, "It's hard not to feel proud of the accomplishments and to feel good about ourselves." Don Kivell agrees:

"Terrific progress is still being made. Over 50 percent of our employees are actively involved in cycle time reduction teams covering our total business cycle from order entry to shipping."

In the best summary of the consequences, Don continues: "It's a paradox. The recession reduced work 25 percent. If we had not come as far as we have in cycle time reduction, we might not be sitting here discussing it. Because of our success, we remain in business. We've been recognized by the head office, and also numerous industries in the region. Despite the business downturn, people still believe in us."

2
The Cycle Time
Management Concept

THE INFLUENCE OF TIME ON PROCESSES

A useful analogy for explaining how time influences a process is to compare the way an average driver changes a tire with the process used by a member of an auto-racing pit crew.

Both the average driver and the pit-crew member have to perform the same functions:

1. Stop the car.
2. Raise the car.
3. Loosen and remove the fastening nut(s).
4. Replace the tire.
5. Tighten the nuts.
6. Lower the car.
7. Go.

If you work fast, have all the tools at hand and in working order, and can loosen the nuts easily, then you can change a tire in 15 minutes. In an Indy 500 or Formula 1 race, however, it is essential to change all tires in less than 15 seconds. A single second can make the difference between winning and losing.

The big difference between the two processes is the idea of measuring both performance and productivity in units of time.

To reduce the time from 15 minutes to 15 seconds requires a plan of what activities are needed and how they must be performed (see Table 2-1). Working out the plan together, team members will appreciate the necessity of carrying out each step in proper order. They will understand that if one person or machine doesn't work properly, the car will sit in pit row and lose any opportunity of winning.

   I. Assemble pit crew and start their training.

  II. Have pit crew develop a plan that defines tasks to be done.
     A. Months in advance
       1. Make car design changes and build jacks into frame.
       2. Research best tires for all conditions.
       3. Assemble and train pit crew.
     B. Day before race
       1. Design and lay out the pit area.
       2. Get proper tires and wrenches to the pit.
       3. Test all equipment to ensure that it is working.
     C. On race day
       1. Ensure that power wrenches are working.
       2. Ensure that tires are at right pressure.
       3. Ensure that each man is at right workstation, with right tires.

  III. Change tires according to plan.

Table 2-1. Plan for Changing a Tire in 15 Seconds

Consider that your company is like the Indy pit crew — in a race against time. To compete successfully you will have to eliminate time-wasting activities. This sounds obvious, but the reality is not so easy to achieve. You will need a new set of management practices to guide you.

Fast-track Cycle Time Management is a process that will help your company reach minimum cycle times in the shortest time possible. It involves all employees in an orderly and continuous process of eliminating nonessential activities.

LINEAR FLOW

In a company managed by cycle time, *people* are the drivers. Their objective is to create a *true linear business flow* that requires *minimum cycle time.* In true linear flow, all functions are interdependent elements of a single process. So that operations flow seamlessly together, the whole process is scheduled as a unit. To accomplish that goal, companies must replace traditional *push* scheduling techniques (see Figure 2-1) with *pull* scheduling processes. For example, to win a relay race, a relay team must perform in true linear flow. The first runner must get a good start, and then at each transfer point both runners must ensure a smooth baton transfer. The objective of each runner is not just to complete his or her leg in the shortest time possible but also to transfer the baton smoothly and with minimal loss of speed. The worst offense is to interrupt the flow by dropping the baton. The usual occurrence is that the receiving runners have to adjust their acceleration to conform to a tiring teammate's speed, thus only marginally interrupting the smooth flow of the team's efforts and maximizing the overall team time. In Chapter 4 we outline the activities that interrupt the linear flow of a business operation.

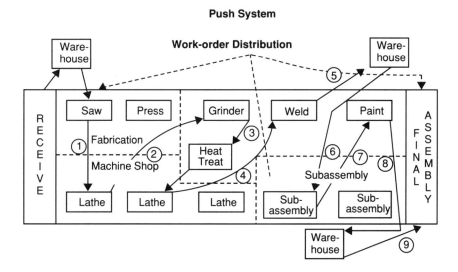

Figure 2-1. Layout of Traditional Plant

Once you consider a company operation as you would a relay race — that is, as a linear process — you can begin to distinguish essential, or value-adding, activities from those that are nonessential, or do not add value.

While some organizations have made progress in reducing manufacturing cycle time, much waste remains in the systems and procedures associated with order entry, engineering, purchasing, internal control, and accounting. Furthermore, most companies that manufacture for a warehouse rather than for direct delivery to the customer have waste in their distribution system. By concentrating on manufacturing alone, you may get manufacturing cycle time down to a week but discover that it takes two months to process the sales order and distribute the product. For example, in 1980 Toyota in Japan found itself needing 7 days to make a car but 14 days to get the order from the customer to the plant and the finished car to the customer. Today it takes 7 days from order to delivery.[1]

SUMMARY OF CTM CONCEPTS

The influence of time, then, is the major difference between traditional operating practices and the CTM approach. CTM encourages workers to distinguish essential from nonessential activities and then to eliminate the nonessential activities. The objective is to create a true linear business flow — from receipt of an order to shipment of goods — that requires minimum cycle time. Also unlike traditional operations, support services such as purchasing, engineering, accounting, and distribution are subjected to a single performance measure — cycle time. Most managers would be able to accept the fact that 90 percent of the activities in their plant do not add value, but they would be shocked to discover that the same percentage holds true in their support services and that more than 60 percent of overall cycle time is taken up by their support systems — from the signing of the sales order to the start of manufacturing. In other words, most of the time spent on the business operation occurs before any value-adding manufacturing activity is performed. It only makes sense, then, to reduce the cycle time required for the entire business operation.

The CTM approach assumes that to reach minimum cycle time you have to involve the real experts — *the workers* — in the process. While outside experts can draw up flowcharts and expose some of the waste, they are unlikely to eliminate all of it. Only the person doing the job knows where *all* of its nonessential activities are located. That is why it is so important for all employees to become involved in the elimination of waste. If they are excluded from the process, some of the waste will certainly remain buried, and, worse, will impede the cycle time reduction process. In CTM, senior managers determine the objective and outline the optimum pace of change; their people, however, will determine the actual pace.

In Chapter 3 we summarize some of the approaches used by companies on the road to CTM. We also show why traditional operating practices are obsolete.

NOTE

1. George Stalk, Jr. and Thomas M. Hout, *Competing Against Time: How Time-Based Competition Is Reshaping Global Markets* (New York: The Free Press, 1990), pp. 67-68.

3

Why Traditional Operating Practices Are Obsolete

In the 1970s, many North American companies were focused on getting control of their operating processes. Materials resources planning (MRP) and manufacturing resources planning (MRPII) systems were developed as methods to improve overall planning and gain control of the manufacturing process. Few companies, however, were able to implement these systems successfully. They gained a better idea of what was going on in their total operation but were unable to translate this information into significant cost reductions. The basic weaknesses of both MRP and MRPII were that they accepted traditional operating practices and never exposed buried waste. Although the investment in materials management feature of MRP and MRPII systems is valuable in CTM, the shop-floor control feature, which is used to schedule individual machines, is not needed. Perhaps that is just as well, since most companies either failed to invest in this feature or had difficulty making it work.

In the mid-1970s, the Japanese invaded the auto and electronics industries. The first reaction of North America manufacturers was to assume that the Japanese were dumping products. Later they complained that the Japanese were using their work-oriented culture and lower wage rates to unfair advantage. Eventually, people caught on to the real reason for the success of Japanese companies: their manufacturing processes were less costly. This realization caused North American manufacturers to rethink what they were doing. To understand their dramatic change in attitude, you first need to understand the assumptions inherent in traditional manufacturing practices.

FEATURES OF THE TRADITIONAL MANUFACTURING OPERATION

The traditional operating assumption is that each department and each machine is a discrete operating unit with its own performance measure and its own schedule. The only way the traditional process can operate is with work-in-process (WIP) inventory buffers of materials between each department or machine, even though everybody knows that inventory is waste. WIP is material on which one value-adding step has been performed yet still requires additional steps before it can be sold as a finished product.

The rationale for using WIP as the line-balancing buffer originated with the misconception that operation changeover times could not be reduced to the point where they were insignificant. Since some machines took considerably longer to change over than others, logic dictated that each machine be treated as a separate entity and pushed to turn out as many units as possible. The goal was high machine and labor utilization.

Clearly, the only way to achieve this goal is to build WIP at each station. The longer the changeover time, the larger the lot size, and, therefore, the larger the WIP. The conception of each support and operating department and each machine as discrete entities has a ripple effect. It leads to an extraordinary buildup of waste that is invisible under existing cost and performance measures. For example, WIP inventories require the following: forklift trucks, which cost $60,000 per unit per year, to move the inventory; warehouse space between machines to store it; computer operators to record its movement through the plant; and other expenses (see Chapter 6).

Plant Layout Is Determined by Function or Available Space

Once machine utilization becomes the driver and each machine is considered to be discrete, it doesn't matter where you locate the machines or departments in the factory. Over time, two common floor plans evolve:

Grouping people and/or machines by function. In the traditional push system of plant layout, the lathes and subassembly are grouped as departments (see Figure 2-1). If you follow the arrows for Steps 1 through 8 you can see how this layout actually increases travel time between functions. You will also note that there are three warehouse boxes in this process. What is not shown is the WIP storage points between each machine acts as the glue enabling this process to work. The time taken to move product between machines as well as the cost of conveyer systems and people to operate the internal distribution systems, including the warehouses, is accepted as built into the process and is thus ignored.

Locating departments or machines wherever there is space. Since time is not a consideration, nobody worries about the amount of travel time. As a result, processes sometimes traverse a company's main building and even spill over into other buildings.

The Company Is Organized by Function

When function becomes a key determinant in setting up the organization, it is logical to divide engineering into process and design. It is also logical to treat maintenance, marketing, purchasing, information systems, and all the service organizations as separate entities. As time goes on, each department and subgroup tends to develop its own performance measures and become a cost center. For example, purchasing starts referring to their in-stock percentages rather than whether production runs out of a particular part. While the length of time required to repair a machine is of interest, the real issue is maintaining machine utilization rates on the other machines.

As the next few sections show, organization by function not only increases cycle time but adds cost to the entire process. Furthermore, none of these costs are exposed by existing performance measures.

WIP Buries Defects

If high machine utilization is the objective, managers have little incentive to shut down a machine to sort out a quality problem. When one piece does not work, the operator or supervisor searches for a usable piece and requests another batch. Batches of defective components resulting from quality problems soon become a fixture in the process. As long as there is WIP, the process exerts no pressure to produce quality parts the first time. The operator's only concern is whether a defective part can be reworked or has to be scrapped. The cost of rework is buried, whereas scrap appears on the manufacturing statement as an expense. As a result, managers tend to accept rework costs and avoid scrap expenses.

Similarly, in the office, as long as the system offers no incentive to do things right the first time, paper flow systems remain inefficient. Suppose that the most basic document — the sales order — is inaccurate and that several people have worked on it before the mistake is discovered. Nobody worries about the rework that the error creates for others. The corrected order is routinely issued and enters the system.

Push as the Traditional Scheduling Approach Creates Complexity

The term *push* was derived because, in general, managers *push* material through machine stations. Ian Ross, a former vice president of manufacturing at Federal Pioneer, suggests that "pushing is also a management style that all too often replaces leadership." Remember that in traditional plants high machine utilization is the goal and each machine is scheduled separately. Therefore, as more machines are added, scheduling becomes increasingly complex. It becomes obvious that existing information systems cannot control the overall process. As a result, computer programs like manufacturing resources planning (MRPII) and, more recently, optimized production technology (OPT), were designed to provide better control of materials and machines and thus of the entire process.

While the new programs have helped to coordinate the activities, they have the significant disadvantage of discouraging productivity improvement, because major program changes are so expensive.

In summary, managers should consider what the push objective of maximizing the output of individual machines without an equal effort to ensure the continuous flow of finished products does to overall plant productivity. During the first three weeks of the month, each machine produces a continuous flow of components, while final assembly is only completing a moderate flow of finished product. Stock shortages, batches of defective components, and machine breakdowns are the usual reasons for this flow disparity. Instead of eliminating the problem immediately, however, the instinct is to muddle on. In the last week, the focus shifts from maximizing machine output to producing finished goods. Productivity and cost considerations become secondary. Instead, you see the following:

- Components and finished units that were previously marginally defective are now acceptable.
- Suppliers are expected to make instant deliveries to cover stock shortages.
- Maintenance personnel are working around the clock to get machines working.
- Operators are working overtime to either rework or replace components that cannot be used.
- Final assembly is on overtime to produce the products.
- Shipping is on overtime to get the product packaged and shipped.

For three weeks of the month, then, there is a process. In the fourth week, hyperactivity replaces productivity. This cycle is repeated month after month and becomes an accepted part of the plant operation. While the actual work of the operators is adding value and is essential, the process required to achieve the objective is adding cost and in many instances creating future costs in the form of warranty rework.

Product Design Is a Marketing Function

In the traditional organization, product design conforms essentially to marketing criteria. The assumption here is that as long as the product is attractive enough to sell and can be manufactured at a competitive cost, then the design criteria has been met. Whether the design can be translated into something that can be manufactured more easily or effectively is someone else's problem. Indeed, manufacturability is a concept that is still new to most North American manufacturers. Moreover, it requires a total reorganization of the engineering function.

Line Operators and Clerical Staff Have No Influence

Although in the traditional operation the operators and clerical people know where waste is buried, their knowledge is largely ignored. Allied to the belief that each machine and department is discrete is the common attitude that the company's brainpower is concentrated in the service departments, such as engineering, accounting, purchasing, and information systems. The traditional job description of the line operators implies that they push buttons and contribute nothing in the way of innovation. The clerical workers' equivalent function is to push paper.

And so the traditional process has continued — logical but wasteful. Why has the waste escaped detection for so long? Standard costing is largely to blame. Consider the three major cost categories in a standard cost system:

- Direct materials (the cost of the raw materials and components used to make the product).
- Direct labor (the wages of those machine operators who are directly involved in adding value to the product).
- Overhead, or burden (the basket in which all other indirect costs accumulate). This includes broad categories such as

indirect labor, general and administrative expenses, and facilities and equipment costs (including depreciation, engineering, and costs associated with materials and inventory).

When you apply standard cost thinking, your attention is focused on lowering your direct costs, which are easily quantifiable in dollars. Since standard cost thinking has no means of recognizing the waste that is buried in overhead, you ignore it.

EARLY EFFORTS TO ELIMINATE WASTE

High Interest Rates Focused Attention on Inventory

In the late 1970s and early 1980s, manufacturers began to feel pressure from high interest rates and offshore competition. As a result, they began to look at costs. Standard cost thinking suggested that they must reduce direct material costs, and this thinking quickly expanded into reducing inventories. As a result, they introduced just-in-time (JIT) manufacturing as an inventory reduction program.

One of the first steps taken by some of the larger manufacturers, particularly those in the auto industry, was to urge suppliers to lower material prices and also force them to hold inventories and to deliver on a just-in-time, or as-needed, basis. It soon became apparent that the suppliers could not absorb the extra cost and survive. Furthermore, while manufacturers saved some cost, it was not nearly as much as expected or required. The only positive outcome of this strategy was that suppliers and customers learned that there were mutual benefits to collaborating on ways of reducing inventories.

To add to the problem, nobody was sure how much inventory was required to operate their plant. They just knew that inventories were essential to the traditional operating system. Most were not aware how much inventory is required to operate a traditional system. When asked why they didn't just eliminate all inventories, manufacturers would answer, "because it would shut down the whole plant." Their reductions provided some savings but not nearly enough to close the gap with offshore competition.

The Focus on Direct Labor

The next major cost area that standard cost thinking suggested needed analysis was direct labor. If focusing on direct materials produced no real savings, focusing on direct labor produced a more serious difficulty for many manufacturers. It seemed that the only way to reduce direct labor was to introduce advanced technologies such as computer-integrated manufacturing (CIM).

General Motors took the high-technology route. Unfortunately for them, the costs were high. Far from the expected shortcut to success, their large investment in CIM dramatically increased depreciation, which reduced both profits and market share. While CIM did reduce direct labor, the General Motors experience demonstrated that reducing direct labor costs — which in most companies are about 8 to 12 percent of total cost — would produce only minimal savings.

Disappointed with these early attempts to reduce waste, manufacturers shifted their attention to two very different approaches.

The Focus on Quality

In the early 1980s, Hewlett-Packard went to its subsidiary in Japan and discovered the concept of *total quality control* (TQC), which soon became known in North America as *total quality commitment*. The aim of TQC is to reduce the number of defects and waste in the total business process. Over the next five years, Hewlett-Packard concentrated on eliminating the causes of defects and waste by changing its processes, and it got some startling results. For example, the facility in Vancouver, Washington, reduced its defects from 4,000 parts per million to 40 to 4. As explained in Chapter 4, CTM also seeks to reduce defects and waste. The major difference between TQC and CTM is that instead of using old performance measures like yields and standard costings to measure productivity and a nebulous phrase like *waste elimination* as its goal, CTM introduces time as the companywide productivity measure and total company cycle time reduction as the finite goal.

The Focused Factory

The focused factory was another attempt to reduce waste created by changeovers and poor work flows. Companies that produced many products explored the idea of creating dedicated lines for each one. They soon realized that it was impractical and uneconomical, both to build separate lines and, to allocate engineers and other service resources to a specific line.

Summary

These diverse approaches to major cost reductions made physical and organizational change acceptable. As people exposed more and more waste across the whole system, they started to see the entire company as one process.

By the mid-1980s external economic factors increased the pressure to improve productivity. Soaring interest rates dictated that all inventories — including WIP, the traditional buffer — had to be dramatically reduced. At the same time, customers started to demand higher-quality products at the same prices for delivery in much shorter time frames. Companies that responded by concentrating on quality and carrying inventory to meet the shorter delivery time requirement soon discovered that they could not absorb the inventory-carrying cost increases.

To meet new customer expectations as well as reduce inventories, companies must

- eliminate the waste in *all* existing systems
- dramatically reduce inventories and their associated costs
- reduce total company cycle time

These objectives are impossible to achieve within traditional systems. With Cycle Time Management, however, all three objectives can be integrated and can converge in *one* total business linear flow process that is managed by cycle time.

4

Total Linear Business Flow

As mentioned in Chapter 2, in a CTM plant *people* are the drivers, and their objective is to create a total business linear flow that requires minimum cycle time. This chapter outlines the rationale for striving for a flow process and the steps necessary to achieve it (see Figure 4-1).

The first step in the evolution to CTM is to introduce the concept of a *total linear business flow process (flow)* throughout the company. Flow is scheduled by customer demand and is the sequence in which paper, drawings, materials, and semicompleted products are moved through the total company process. In flow, materials, paper, and the like move continuously, stopping only when value is being added or an essential activity is being performed.

In contrast to the traditional assumption that each machine and function is a discrete operating unit, the basic assumption of flow is that when one machine is down, all machines are down. In this environment each machine, in fact each function, is interdependent. Teamwork and good communications at all levels are therefore essential. Flow goes beyond manufacturing to include service departments, such as order entry, purchasing, engineering, distribution, and accounting.

If your company has already adopted other popular approaches and techniques, they can be integrated with CTM. For example, just-in-time (JIT) manufacturing practices and strategies are used to expose non-value-adding activities, or nonessential activities, as we

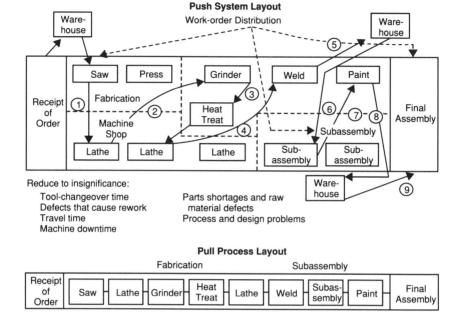

**Figure 4-1. Steps for Transforming Traditional Plant to Pull
Process Layout**

call them in CTM. The concept of pull scheduling is also derived from JIT techniques. Total quality management (TQM) approaches are used to identify quality defects and other waste. Statistical process control (SPC) techniques are used to determine deviations from expected results. Computer-integrated manufacturing (CIM) and other technological concepts have their place as well. Flow provides the rationale for a coordinated effort to:

- reduce changeovers to minutes or seconds
- eliminate travel times between value-adding steps in both service and manufacturing operations
- eliminate rework rather than burying it
- integrate the engineering functions of design, process, and maintenance to improve manufacturability, machine reliability, and uptime

Once flow becomes your objective, you become focused on exposing the impediments to achieving it. These impediments are buried in the following areas:

1. The Manufacturing Process
   * tool changeovers
   * poor quality that creates rework
   * parts shortages and poor materials that cause downtime
   * plant layout that creates travel time
   * poor maintenance procedures that cause downtime
   * poor process and design engineering that causes poor quality
2. Support Services
   * sales order changes
   * engineering changes
   * clerical delays
   * travel time
   * office equipment and tools downtime
   * distribution

SCHEDULING — MOVING FROM PUSH TO PULL

The pull thinking process provides a rationale and incentive to eliminate impediments. It is valuable to introduce the thinking process at the start, even though you will not be able to implement pull scheduling until most of the impediments are removed. To move a plant from push to pull, you must ensure that all employees receive sufficient training. Everybody must be aware of what a pull system looks like and understand both the thinking and operating practices associated with it. Simulation games, such as the JIT game, can help people to understand pull thinking.

Imagine a piece of rope that is three feet long. Start at one end and push it. The rope just crumbles into a jumble of coils and confusion. Now start at the same end and pull the rope. It soon straightens out and becomes totally controlled by the pressure at the front end.

The pressure for production planners in both push and pull systems is customer demand. In the push system, however, only sales and scheduling feel the pressure of customer demand. To operators and the other manufacturing functions, the real pressure is the artificial goal of maximizing the output of each machine and building sufficient inventories to meet any and all customer needs. Therefore, each machine and final assembly must be scheduled separately, while the outputs must be controlled and moved from function to function as discrete operations. The flow of this process becomes as jumbled as the rope that is being pushed.

By contrast, in pull scheduling, customer demand provides the pressure throughout the process. In pull, each workstation and support function serve as both an internal customer and a supplier. From an operator's perspective, the difference between the two systems is suggested by Figure 4-2.

The flow of materials remains the same in both push and pull, however, the flow of scheduling information is quite different. To better understand this difference, consider the Machine 2 operators in the pull system. They will no longer have their own schedule, so their attention will switch from the pile of WIP containers being *pushed* from their supplier (Machine 1) to meeting the demands of their customer (Machine 3). In practice, the sale of one unit of product triggers a demand at Machine 3 to *pull* another unit through Machine 2, which in turn triggers a demand for Machine 1 to produce another unit. In that way, customer demand ripples through each individual station throughout the entire process.

Pull thinking must now be translated into practices for daily scheduling of the operations. The most common practice is to develop a personalized variation on the kanban system introduced by Toyota Motor in the early 1950s.

THE ROLE OF KANBAN IN A PULL SYSTEM

Kanban is the Japanese word for "card." The kanban card is an authorization from a customer to a supplier to make either one unit or a small number of units. (Assume that we are talking about

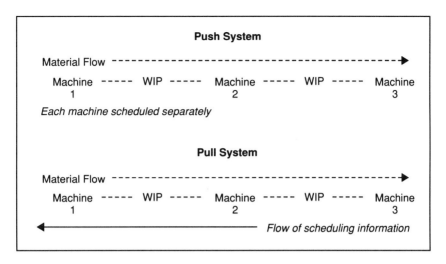

Figure 4-2. Difference Between Push and Pull Systems

internal customers and suppliers at this point.) Then the kanban card authorizes each internal supplier to refurbish his or her customer's WIP. This may be stored in a marked area on the floor, a bin, or some other container.

To avoid the perception traditionally associated with WIP, we shall from now on refer to it as kanban. In a traditional system, WIP hides the waste and is an accepted part of the process. In a pull system, the kanban is an indicator of waste that can be eliminated. It is assumed that as the waste is reduced, the kanban size will also go down. The ideal number for a kanban is three, but it is seldom reached.

On the first day of the transition from push to pull, the quantity in each kanban will be the same as the WIP in the old process. In addition, the first kanban cards will authorize a number that probably corresponds to the prevailing batch size at each station.

In a pull system that uses the kanban concept, each kanban card is a customer/operator authorization to a supplier/operator to make and deliver a quantity of material or components to their kanban.

Let's go through the kanban operating process step by step:

1. The flow starts when an external customer buys a unit of finished product and the unit is shipped.
2. The kanban card from the shipped unit is returned to scheduling, thus setting the internal pull system in motion.
3. At the appropriate time, final assembly receives a kanban card authorizing them to make a unit of product.
4. Final assembly pulls the necessary quantity of material or components from their kanban forward into their work area, attaches the kanban cards to each component or piece of material, and sends the work back to the appropriate machine operator or materials area.
5. The card authorizes each internal supplier to supply. When the kanban quantity has been made, the material and its accompanying kanban card are moved to the internal customer's kanban area, and the supplier workstation stops producing that unit.
6. If the station gets another kanban card authorizing it to make a different component, the operator does a changeover and proceeds to produce this component.

Rather than building for stock, as is the tradition in push systems, operators in pull systems build only what is required by the kanban card or demanded by the customer. As soon as the demand is met, they either change over and fulfill the demand on the next kanban card or *they stop the machine.* No doubt the implications of scheduling with kanban cards have already become clear to the reader. Obviously, it is much simpler than scheduling each machine, but it is a new approach and demands discipline on the part of each individual. Since discipline requires understanding, training for all personnel is essential.

A number of things become clear once operators start to think in terms of the pull system. For example, they quickly see that long changeovers require large kanbans and impede their ability to respond quickly to customer requests. Similarly, they realize that their flexibility is reduced and larger kanbans are necessary wherever the flow is impeded by long travel times between machines or processes, or by defects due to poor quality defects or constant machine breakdowns. It also becomes obvious that functions such as purchasing, engineering, and accounting must be integrated into the process. Finally, as they eliminate the impediments they discover that

- kanbans, which are inventories, can be reduced
- cycle times go down
- costs that are associated with kanbans and have been buried in overheads are reduced
- complex and discrete traditional systems are merged into one smooth linear business flow

As you get closer to the ideal of flow, you can see the sense of replacing forecast with customer demand as a means of determining the quantity, mix, and timing of products to be made. One General Electric plant, after reducing its cycle time from six weeks to one week, eliminated the forecast of how many brown-sided refrigerators with the freezer on the left-hand side were needed and simply built them to order.[1] Now you have a strong incentive to concentrate on locating and eliminating the impediments in both the manufacturing process and the support services.

THE MANUFACTURING PROCESS

Tool Changeovers

In this section, we use *tool* as a generic term for dies, jigs, fixtures, cradles, and any other tools used in a traditional changeover. Tools also include molds and vats that are part of the process industry.

If you have any long tool changeovers, you must stop ignoring them as necessary costs. Instead, recognize them as major impediments to achieving flow and root them out.

There are two ways to reduce changeovers. You can use a totally dedicated machine, or you can concentrate on trying to reduce changeovers to a single minute. Either way you will not only reduce cycle time but you will also eliminate the WIP that was previously required to buffer the changeover time.

Consider these examples: A Blount subsidiary, formerly called Omark Industries, made marked reductions in setup time on its 250-ton Pacific press, where die changes were averaging four hours. Previously, the 275-kilo die inserts had been moved by a crane, a forklift truck, and two additional workers. Omark eliminated adjustment time — which accounted for about 50 percent of the total time — by creating a single-size outside dimension for all dies, and welding guides on each machine for "one size fits all" die installation, thus creating a fail-safe insertion process. To store the dies, the company built movable trolleys beside the presses and set up a system of air hoses to simplify any lifting required by the change. Finally, for all dies it designed a set of fast-attach and quick-release clamps. As a result, one person can now change a die in approximately 50 seconds.[2]

At Black and Decker, the engineers removed all allowances for changeovers. Now setups are charged to each department as variances. The result is that there is a sense of urgency to reduce changeovers. In one department, it took two people two and a half hours to change a mold. Through training and videotaping, operators have lowered that time by nearly 50 percent.[3]

Poor organization of time is the usual cause of delays in changeovers. Recall the earlier contrast between the 15-minute tire change and the 10- to 15-second times of the skilled racing pit crews. The key is to determine the essential changeover activities, when and how they must be performed, and then how to eliminate the nonessential activities.

At the Kawasaki Motors subsidiary in Lincoln, Nebraska, an operator used to take three hours to do one setup. After modifying their machine for quick changeovers, the operator was doing 14 changeovers in the same three-hour period (or about 1 changeover every 12 minutes).[4] A machine obviously has to be stopped to change a die. The question is, *for how long?* Remember, in a CTM operation machine downtime is a critical factor.

There is an easy process for your changeover to follow:

1. Make a videotape of the present changeover process.
2. Divide the activities into external (activities that can be done *before* the machine is stopped) and internal (activities

that can be done only *after* the machine is stopped).

3. Try to eliminate the nonessential activities and simplify the existing process.

4. Move as many internal activities as possible to the external category.

When several machines have long changeovers, you start with the machine that creates the largest bottleneck and then proceed down the line.

The details of how to reduce changeover times are not addressed in this book. The point is that the objective of Single-Minute Exchange of Die (SMED) is not only possible — as Shigeo Shingo has shown[5] — but essential to developing flow and reducing cycle time.

Poor Quality That Creates Rework

In a traditional operation the process exerts no internal pressure to build a quality product on the first pass, because the cost of poor quality can be ignored and buried in WIP as long as the material can be reworked. Only the cost of writing off the materials is recorded.

In the CTM process, by contrast, defects in quality are unacceptable for two reasons. First, rework destroys the flow of the whole factory process. Second, since lot sizes are very small, a defective piece will quickly stop the whole line because the next station will be unable to do its job. As a result, when defects do appear, *the process itself* exerts pressure to uncover and eradicate the cause of the defect as quickly as possible.

Aside from disrupting the whole process, rework causes a series of delays and nonessential activities such as special handling, storing, and recording activities, all of which dramatically increase cycle time.

Managers used to assume that people were the cause of quality problems. That was before experts such W. Edwards Deming, Philip Crosby, and Joseph Juran demonstrated that the process itself accounts for about 85 percent of quality problems. These men linked quality control to the larger concept of total quality management (TQM) and put the spotlight on the whole company process, thus including diverse functions such as defective materials, incorrect drawings, poor procedures, erroneous information, and unnecessary paperwork.

The initial quality problems emanate from poorly defined or non-existent standards in key areas such as:

- poor product design, which encourages the need for "crowbar and rubber hammer" solutions
- engineering changes that are not coordinated into the whole system and lead to a wide range of tolerances and other types of quality problems
- poor equipment and tool maintenance, which leads to tolerance changes that cause defects

Poor quality also is caused by push-oriented managers who want production volume even if that requires out-of-tolerance concessions to be made so that production stoppages can be avoided.

Measuring Quality. When the process problems are uncovered, the next step is to reassess the definition of quality to ensure that it conforms to customer requirements. The highest quality is attained when you meet your customers' requirements 100 percent of the time. The requirements must involve more than visible attractiveness; they must be *measurable*. When product and process quality becomes measurable, then and only then does it become possible to think about zero defects.

To underline the importance of *meeting customer requirements* let's look at a simple example. A quality speaker for one auto company used to include the specification of being able to play under water. Regardless of how impractical this requirement was, to make a 100 percent quality speaker the manufacturer had to meet it. When the job was put out for tender the new supplier asked if the speaker really had to work under water. As a result of this questioning, the customer removed the requirement from its specifications. The supplier was able to make a 100 percent quality radio at half the cost and got the order.

A more serious example of creating rework because customer specifications are not being met has caught one Canadian manufacturer in a dispute about who should pay the $300,000 cost of redesigning and rebuilding a die. For several years, the client produced a product that did not meet exactly the customer specifications. The client got away with the error since the customer had a simple way of reworking the component at its own plant. However, when the customer designed and built a new factory, the engineers built the new process to take components that conformed to the original specifications and now refused to accept the nonconforming parts. Why were the specifications not met from the start? The question is, who determines whether quality standards have been met? In a traditional process, the external customer and internal inspectors have that responsibility. In a CTM operation, the inspection function is performed by two customers. The *external,* or *final, customer* who orders the finished product remains the final arbiter. The quality inspector also remains the final internal judge of quality. The goal today, however, is to transfer most of the responsibility for quality to the *internal customer.* This is the person who builds on the previous workstation's efforts in the linear business flow process, either on the shop floor or in the office.

The need for quality control inspectors is thus greatly reduced in the CTM organization because building in quality has become the job of all employees, whether they are producing paperwork, a single component, or a finished product. For example, Camco, a Canadian subsidiary of General Electric, has been able to reduce its number of inspectors to 3 from a high of 25.[6] If the incoming part or information does not meet the customer's requirements, then it must be rejected and the cause of the problem rooted out.

A properly trained CTM work force uses tools such as statistical process controls (SPC), and cause-and-effect (sometimes called fishbone) diagrams to root out the causes of defects that are producing delays in the whole process. These and other CTM tools are described in more detail in Chapter 8.

The purpose of these tools is, first, to identify that there is a problem or deviation from standard and, second, to note and chart the number of occurrences. Rather than working from an opinion that a problem exists, you work from charts and diagrams that document the number of occurrences and direct you beyond superficial causes to the root cause. Moreover, use of the charts banishes workers' concern that in identifying a problem they are blowing the whistle on a colleague. Instead, it encourages them to work as a group toward the common goal of reducing cycle time. They do this by ridding the system of processes that cause defects or create delays.

Neither objective — that of reducing cycle time or eliminating defects — can be met if you fail to provide workers with leadership and proper training. As explained in Chapters 6 and 7, everybody must learn, for example, that the analytical tools used to expose quality problems can also be used to reduce cycle time. People must also learn, for example, how to work in groups to achieve their common goals.

Parts Shortages and Poor Materials
That Cause Downtime

External suppliers are often singled out in quality improvement programs because they can be a major cause of both increased downtime and defects in the quality process. Yet the defects they create are most often caused by the same poorly defined requirements and inattention to standards that afflict the internal process.

When companies have documented their requirements and standards and can demonstrate their own commitment to internal quality improvement and to achieving cycle time reduction, then it is time to develop partnerships with key suppliers under the umbrella of supply management. Approached in the right spirit, most suppliers want to cooperate, and many have good ideas about how to improve quality.

Plant Layout That Creates Travel Time

You will not be able to create a smooth linear flow until you reduce travel time between machines, processes, and departments and balance machine outputs throughout the process.

Travel Time. Visualize what your operation would look like if all the machines were laid out by process instead of by function, and if there was no travel time between machines nor any delays because a towmotor, crane, or elevator was not immediately available. Don't limit yourself to a straight-line flow. It may, for example, be appropriate to set up several machines in a U-cell (see Figure 4-3). This layout is particularly appropriate if the output of the cell is variable. On some days line balancing requirements may dictate that you have one operator per machine; on others you may have one person operating more than one machine in the cell.

The experience of Blount's plant in Guelph, Ontario, demonstrates the impact that changes in plant layout can have in some

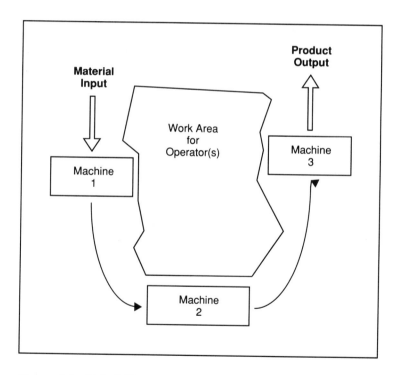

Figure 4-3. U-Cell Diagram

processes. The company actually shortened the distance in its bar department — from 2,620 feet to 173 feet.[7] If your operation comprises several plants, you may find that you can consolidate them. Blount was able to relocate a complete factory in the excess space created by the company's transition.

IBM's Owego, New York, plant was able to reduce the distance of their line from 31,000 to 275 feet.[8] As you reduce the delays caused by plant layout, you see reductions in both cycle time and costs. For example, you reduce or eliminate

- the WIP required to buffer the travel times
- costs associated with conveyers and transporting vehicles
- the costs of their operating and maintenance crews
- the cost of floor space around the machines

Line balancing. When travel time is reduced, line balancing surfaces as another impediment to achieving flow. Remember that in flow all functions and machines are *interdependent*: the process can produce only as much as the lowest-output machine or work cell. As a result, balancing the line becomes an essential scheduling consideration. Two approaches are used to balance a CTM line. The first is the occasional shutdown of the high-output machines. The second is to increase the outputs of bottleneck machines.

Scheduling the bottleneck machine is the critical line-balancing issue. The first job, obviously, is to identify the bottleneck machine — the one that produces the lowest output in the process. The low output may be due to low capacity, slow speeds, frequent breakdowns, or all of these factors. Whatever the reason, you need to manage this machine in order to increase the output of the whole process. Any of the following actions might relieve a bottleneck:

- Train more operators and keep the machine operating longer.
- Set up a special preventive maintenance program to enable the machine to run with fewer breakdowns.
- Set up an old machine as a dedicated machine running in parallel, even if it runs at a slower rate.

- Purchase a new machine.

As cycle time decreases, other bottlenecks will surface. For example, after Hewlett-Packard reduced its cycle time from 42 to 2 days, it was the credit system that initially prevented it from going down to 1 day.

When you have eliminated the impediments resulting from changeovers, defects, and layout, the schedulers can start to reduce lot sizes and to implement pull techniques.

Poor Maintenance Procedures That Cause Downtime

Because machine downtime is unacceptable in a CTM operation, maintenance is crucial. Proper maintenance procedures ensure that

- operators perform basic preventive maintenance (PM) as part of their jobs
- special PM programs are developed for bottleneck machines
- an inventory of vital parts is taken
- machine reliability is increased dramatically through
  — better training of operators
  — analysis of maintenance history data
  — use of predictive and diagnostic tools
  — improvement of key-part accessibility
- purchase more reliable machines with more maintenance-free parts
- more planned maintenance is performed
- ease of maintenance becomes a criterion in the equipment evaluation process

Perhaps the best way to explain new versus old thinking on maintenance is to tell this simple story: A supervisor of one small process is concerned about one of his key bottleneck machines. If this machine's main bearing breaks, it will take five days to repair, but it will also take five days to determine how much wear has already occurred. This supervisor decides to wait until that machine breaks down before replacing the bearing.

Faced with the same situation, a CTM manager immediately makes a plan. He or she forms a team of operators, maintenance workers, and engineers to create the replacement process. One of the team's first objectives is to determine whether it is possible to shorten the repair period. Suppose they discover that they can change the bearing in three days instead of five: Now the manager can plan to minimize the impact of the downtime by doing the job on a long weekend or during a planned shutdown long before there is a chance of a breakdown due to wear and tear.

Poor Process and Design Engineering That Causes Poor Quality

The engineers must be intimately involved in all phases of cycle time reduction because they must control the product and process design changes. Their basic role should be as resources or advisers to project teams, not necessarily as leaders.

In addition to their work on cycle time reduction project teams, the engineers will play a major role in achieving the second cycle time reduction stage, which is to drive down processing time toward zero cycle time.

There are three ways to reduce processing times:

- with group technology
- by reducing the number of processing steps
- by reducing the number of components in products

Most people are already aware of the cycle time reduction opportunities that technology makes possible; just starting to be recognized, however, is the impact of reducing processing steps or the number of components. Design for manufacturability (DFM) has the potential to produce major cycle time reductions since assembly, while only a part of the process, accounts for about two-thirds of the manufacturing cost. Just cutting back on the number of screws, nuts and bolts, and other fasteners can chop 50 percent or more from assembly costs.

The following experiences demonstrate the impact of process and product design improvements on cycle time reduction:

- General Electric reduced the number of parts in one of its refrigerator compressors from 51 to 29 by simply switching from a reciprocating to a rotary compressor.[9]
- IBM has developed a printer with 65 percent fewer parts and as a result has been able to slash assembly time by 90 percent, to only three minutes.[10]
- Chrysler's van wagon has only 3 body styles (the J-cars and M-cars had 10) and 50 percent fewer parts than its predecessors.[11]
- Geoffrey Boothroyd and Peter Dewhurst, two engineering professors at Rhode Island University, have developed a computer program that analyzes and simplifies all the parts that go into a product. According to *Business Week,* "Companies such as Ford have used it to slash the number of parts in door assemblies and Xerox has used it to make its low-end copiers more competitive." [12]

Recently, more engineering groups have realized that their own internal systems were becoming bottlenecks in cycle time reduction and started to develop internal processes such as simultaneous engineering to address the issue. Its purpose is to integrate key functions such as engineering, production, and purchasing with the customer from the start of the project. Henry W. Stoll describes the process with his *4 Cs:*

1. *Concurrence:* Product and process design run in parallel and occur in the same time frame.
2. *Constraints:* Process constraints are considered part of the product design. This helps ensure that parts are easy to fabricate, handle, and assemble and facilitates use of simple cost-effective process, tooling, and material-handling solutions.
3. *Coordination:* Product and process are closely coordinated so that there is optimal matching of needs and requirements for effective cost, quality, and delivery.
4. *Consensus:* High-impact product and process decision-making involve full team participation and consensus.[13]

Ingersoll Milling Machine (Rockford, Illinois) has used this approach to involve their customers in the whole process — starting with the design of the machine. Here are some figures that

John B. Droy, the vice president of simultaneous engineering, uses: In 1978, the company built a transfer line for machining in-line, four-cylinder engine blocks. That project involved 62 customer-initiated changes at a cost of $1.3 million. In 1988, Ingersoll completed a vee-type block line for the same customer. Using simultaneous engineering, it completed the new line with only seven changes at a cost of $436,000. Ingersoll calculates the process saved another $750,000 in modifications to customer specifications.

In cycle time terms, the 1988 project took 23 weeks less time than the one in 1978 and saved another $750,000.[14] Changeover, quality, travel, parts shortages, maintenance, and engineering all affect the flow of physical materials and components through the shop process.

Engineering is just one of the support functions that affects total business linear flow and cycle time. Another pool of buried cost becomes apparent when companies look beyond the physical flow of materials and components through their manufacturing process at their total cycle time. This source of hidden cost is the other manufacturing support systems.

SUPPORT SERVICES

These support functions have been described as "unreconstructed bastions of the old bad habits of excessive compartmentalization and tunnel vision, with predictable results in bureaucracy, delay, and 'invisible inventory.'"[15] There are several categories of support functions:

- those that are performed before manufacturing adds any value
- distribution, which performs its job after the manufacturing process
- accounting, the scorekeeper for flow (see Chapter 7)

The aim of support services is to determine

- what information is essential
- the activities required to produce that information

- how to accelerate the flow of information by eliminating the nonessential activities that are buried in the various support processes

To see the nonessential activities buried in support systems in perspective, consider the experience of Toyota. In 1982 the automaker could make a car in 2 days, but it needed 15 to 26 days to close the sale, process the order, and deliver the finished car to the customer. That process cost more than it cost to manufacture the car itself. By 1987, Toyota had reduced the system responsiveness from order to delivery to any point in Japan to eight days, including the time required to make the car.[16] Toyota's experience is not unusual: the same ratio of support to manufacturing shows up in most traditional operations.

The support functions are a vital part of the total process because they prepare the information (such as sales orders and engineering drawings) that keeps the process moving. Since they have not been subjected to time pressure or a simple productivity measure, support service activities have never been questioned.

Most system-generated waste is the result of treating each support function as a discrete cost center. Over time, this practice encourages people to "throw problems over the wall" to the next group. Westinghouse Corporate Quality Centre studies show that nearly two-thirds of quality-failure costs are due to white-collar issues — not factory problems. They also note that the biggest total quality improvements are coming from the sales and order-entry offices, the drafting rooms and designers' cubicles, and the credit people who collect receivables.[17] It must be stated also that we are not accusing individuals of wasting their time. As Deming and others have pointed out in the context of quality improvement, it is the *system* that creates unnecessary activities for individuals. An occurrence at KeepRite demonstrates that point. Penny Pickering points out that three years ago, there were five women entering data in her department, and they always had a large backlog of paper on hand. Today after switching to CTM, "I do this same work myself in two hours each day and have time to upgrade my computer skills and prepare little programs on the PC for others to use."

The Key Information Flow Process

Flow starts with the key information that comes from the sales order process. The first requirement is to ensure that the company can meet the customer's expectations for quality, quantity, design, price, and delivery date. When the sales order is signed, the customer expectations need to be translated into manufacturing information and relayed to each of three groups:

1. *Engineering* needs the information to determine first, whether new or existing drawings will be required, and second, what information must be relayed to production control.

2. *Purchasing* needs to know what its supplier network will need to produce and when. Unlike the other functions, purchasing depends on an external network of suppliers that traditionally are not as easily controlled. To overcome this weakness more and more companies are reducing the number of their suppliers and forming partnerships with them. As part of this new relationship, suppliers are expected to:
   - help improve the design of their components if they are supplying components
   - respond to internal kanban cards, which will necessitate more frequent deliveries of smaller quantities
   - help work out any logistical problems that these new delivery requirements create

   Planning and coordination between purchasing and each supplier is vital to achieving flow and reducing cycle time.

3. *Production control* needs the sales order and engineering and purchasing information to plan the production schedule. Although the pull system reduces scheduling problems, manufacturing cannot start its processes until it has the basic information provided by the other support services.

To reduce overall cycle time, each of these functions must look critically at its internal procedures as well as the whole process, and eliminate the causes of delays.

Sales Order Changes

A change to the sales order can cause rework in every function in the company because it triggers activities in every function required to produce the product.

For example, to shorten cycle time a custom manufacturer in Canada often issued the sales order to purchasing, engineering, and production control before the customer had signed it. Inevitably, the customers made changes, which meant that all the documents had to be recalled and reissued. Reissuing the sales order created a ripple effect of rework: Purchasing had to make changes to some of their purchase orders and engineering often had to redo some of their drawings. This company eliminated many hours of rework with the simple decision that no sales order would be circulated to any internal department until the customer's signature was on it.

Engineering Changes

Unlike the sales order changes, engineering changes will always be a part of the total operating process. Nevertheless, they too are a source of rework. The most consistent cause of rework is a failure to keep the information on subordinate documents synchronized with the main engineering data base or the drawings. For example, the bill of material sometimes shows information that differs from the most recent engineering drawing. In the traditional organization, people resolve the problem over time. In CTM, however, this lack of coordination can interrupt the whole process.

Consider the following example of how poor transmission of engineering information disrupted flow and increased cycle time: An auto parts company in Cambridge, Ontario, lost an experienced operator to retirement. During the transition all drawings that had accumulated around this person's machine were thrown out. Within a few days, this station started to turn out poor-quality components. The reason was that the engineering changes that had been documented informally on those drawings over the years had never been formally incorporated on the masters.

The length of time necessary to make engineering changes can be another source of waste. How many people have to approve engineering changes, and how easy is it to get in touch with them? Let's look at the cycle time involved in a simple engineering change at Pratt & Whitney. It involved mounting an engine a fraction of a millimeter closer to the fuselage than the blueprint specified. To start the process an engineer had to develop a submission, which required a mountain of paper. Then the submission had to wind its way through nine departments and a committee that met only once per week. To solve the problem, Pratt & Whitney gave the design engineer the decision, and now only three signatures are required before a change can go through. The engineering cycle time dropped from 82 to 10 days, and the request backlog has shrunk from 1,900 to fewer than 100.[18]

Clerical Delays

Consider what circumstances make it impossible for clerks to complete their work in one pass or without delays. For example, does purchasing have to reach a person at the vendor's business to place an order, or is a fax sufficient? If the order is marked "rush," is a telephone call needed? In the case of engineering, does the blueprinting process or any other procedure create a bottleneck anywhere in the flow? For example, one engineering group discovered that it lost two days as a result of having its blueprints made outside the company.

Do the present capital budgeting approval procedures impede the linear business flow? A certain textile company discovered this impediment. It took so long to get all the signatures necessary to approve the capital for the plant layout changes that the whole cycle time reduction process was delayed.

Travel Time

One order-entry improvement team we worked with videotaped the entire journey a typical order made through the company. They found that it took about seven days for an order to travel 6,200 feet. After the team studied the videotape, they were able to reduce the number of days to six. Today, the use of electronic mail concepts has whittled down cycle time to two days.

Office Equipment and Tools Downtime

Manufacturing support functions such as purchasing, engineering, and production control depend on several types of machines. Computers, photocopiers, and air-conditioning are essential to each function. Engineering may also rely on blueprinting machines.

Would a breakdown in any of these machines affect the present process? If the cycle time is reduced to two or three days, would a breakdown in any of these machines create a bottleneck?

Distribution

In some companies distribution is an extension of the marketing function; in others, it is an extension of manufacturing. If the goods are delivered to a warehouse rather than directly to the customer, the traditional tendency is to make the warehouse an extension of marketing.

If you have a long cycle time, you may have to hold finished goods inventories to meet customer response time demands. As you shorten the overall cycle time, however, the warehouse function will be greatly reduced or eliminated.

	Before CTM	After CTM	Percent Reduction
Harley-Davidson motorcycles	360 days	< 3 days	99%
Motor controllers	56 days	7 days	88%
Electric components	24 days	1 day	96%
Radar detectors	22 days	3 days	86%

Table 4-1. Typical Improvements in Cycle Time Flows

If your company did the same, would it still need an elaborate distribution system to meet your customer response times? At this point, it should be clear where the impediments to flow are buried in both the manufacturing process and the support functions. Let us now examine the role that inventory plays as the impediments disappear.

WIP'S ROLE IN THE WAR ON WASTE

In traditionally managed businesses, WIP was regarded as wasteful but unavoidable, because it was the glue that held the process together. Once you think in terms of flow, pull, and kanbans, however, you get a different idea of inventory.

Inventory is essential to buffer

- the impediments to flow that are found in the traditional functions of transit, queues, changeovers, inspections, and waits
- waste that is caused by quality defects, machine breakdowns, poor design, and process
- long order-entry processes, cumbersome engineering change processes, and other wasteful practices

In other words, WIP signals where the impediments are buried. Once you eliminate the impediment, you can reduce WIP. (Obviously, if you reduce WIP before eliminating the nonessential activities, you will eventually close down the whole process.) The reduction of WIP is yet another bonus for achieving flow.

Many companies, anxious to reduce customer response time have already eliminated a great deal of waste. They have also reduced inventories somewhat. However, most are plodding by comparison to what they could accomplish if they changed their operating practices and began to manage by cycle time.

NOTES

1. Thomas A. Stewart, "GE Keeps Those Ideas Coming," *Fortune,* 12 August 1991, p. 48.
2. Herbert Wedderburn, "The Hidden Sins of Safety Stock," *Industrial Management,* July 1985, p. 46.
3. Walter E. Goddard, *Just-in-Time: Surviving by Breaking Tradition* (Essex Junction, VT: Oliver Wight Publications, 1986), p.70.
4. Richard J. Schonberger, *Japanese Manufacturing Techniques: Nine Hidden Lessons in Simplicity* (New York: The Free Press, 1982) p. 109.
5. Shigeo Shingo, *A Revolution in Manufacturing: The SMED System* (Cambridge: Productivity Press, 1986).
6. Ross Laver, "Scrapping the Assembly Line: Camco Adopts a New Mindset," *Maclean's Magazine,* 12 August 1991, p. 29.
7. Wedderburn, p. 46.
8. Richard J. Schonberger, *World Class Manufacturing: The Lessons of Simplicity Applied* (New York: The Free Press, 1986), p. 231.
9. Bruce Nussbaum, "Smart Design Quality Is the New Style," *Business Week,* 11 April 1988, p. 105.
10. Ibid., p. 105.
11. Schonberger, *Japanese Manufacturing Techniques,* p. 146.
12. Nussbaum, p. 185.
13. Robert N. Stauffer, "Converting Customers to Partners at Ingersoll," *Manufacturing Engineering,* September 1988, p. 43.
14. Ibid., p. 41.
15. Simon Caulkin and Ingersoll Engineers, *The New Manufacturing: Minimal IT for Maximum Profit* (London: The Economist Publications, February 1989), p. 101.
16. Stalk and Hout, p. 48.
17. Caulkin, et al., p. 102.
18. Todd Vogel, "Where 1990-Style Management Is Already Hard at Work," *Business Week,* 23 October 1989, p. 96.

5

Cycle Time as the
Measure for Productivity

Achieving total business linear flow will obviously reduce customer response time. However, like the relay team, the productivity team needs a time goal if it is to reduce response time quickly and continuously.

CYCLE TIME VERSUS *LEAD TIME?*

The terms *lead time* and *cycle time* have different meanings. *Lead time* is a scheduling tool. As well, it encourages a distorted perspective of productivity, because once established a lead time tends to become cast in stone. To calculate lead time you start with the delivery date and then work backward with a series of time estimates through all support and manufacturing functions, to determine the start time needed to meet the delivery date. The lead time calculation includes processing time as well as buffers for delays. Some companies also include a buffer called *safety time.*

Cycle time, on the other hand, is not a scheduling tool but a *productivity improvement measure.* While on day one of the transition, cycle time and lead time might be the same, the cycle time calculation is based on two assumptions that distinguish it from lead time. First, in the cycle time model there are no buffers because they create delays and are not essential to the manufacturing process. Second, cycle time is a moving standard that is constantly reduced.

The difference between a lead time and a cycle time model for a machine cell on the shop floor demonstrates the difference between cycle time and lead time thinking (see Figure 5-1).

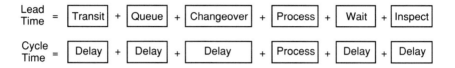

Figure 5-1. Machine Cell: How Lead Time Activities Are Viewed in Cycle Time Thinking

The model can be modified for clerical jobs in any operation (see Figure 5-2).

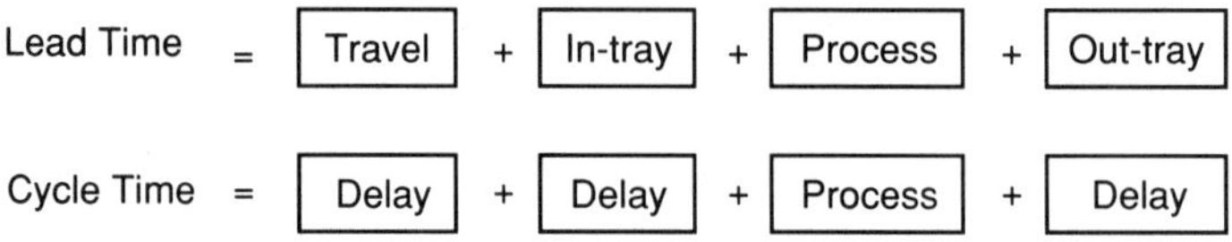

Lead Time = Travel + In-tray + Process + Out-tray

Cycle Time = Delay + Delay + Process + Delay

Figure 5-2. Support Services: How Lead Time Activities Are Viewed in Cycle Time Thinking

Since the assumptions associated with lead time and cycle time are so different, we suggest that companies abandon the phrase *lead time* in order to avoid confusion.

It is inevitable that managers will begin by seeing total company cycle time as a series of interacting subcycles, which can be depicted as gears (see Figure 5-3). This reflects the layout of their departments as separate units.

Eventually, however, they must give up this perspective on cycle time. Instead, they should visualize each function — each job — as an integral part of the total business cycle time.

One of the benefits of using cycle time as the measure for productivity is that time is the one element common to all jobs, no matter what their nature. Indeed, it is a common value in western culture itself. As soon as time is introduced as a measure, people automatically try to reduce it. On the job some people will

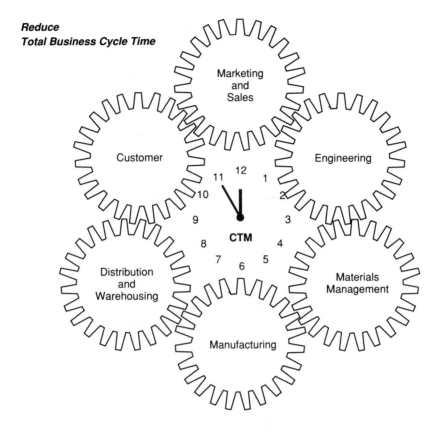

Figure 5-3. The Interacting Subcycles of a Company

endeavor to work faster. Others will begin analyzing their daily activities to determine which ones might be eliminated.

BUILDING CYCLE TIME GOALS

The first revelation from any activity analysis is that only two types of activities occur in every job throughout the company:

- Activities that are essential and add value (these account for about 10 percent of the total activities)
- Activities that are nonessential, impede flow and add cost (these account for the remaining 90 percent)

Cycle time can be shown as an equation for the total business (see Figure 5-4).

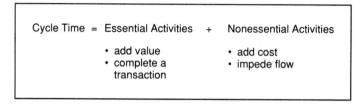

Cycle Time = Essential Activities + Nonessential Activities

               • add value   • add cost
               • complete a   • impede flow
                  transaction

Figure 5-4. Two Components of Cycle Time

DETERMINE THE INITIAL CYCLE TIME

To be able to chart your successes, you first need to estimate your *baseline*, which represents your present cycle time. Assume for this rough estimate that it is the same as your present lead time. Don't spend too much time trying to come up with an exact figure, since as much as 90 percent of the activities in the process are nonessential and will be eliminated quickly anyway. (As the nonessentials disappear, a more precise cycle time will emerge.) To move from baseline cycle time you must stage a sequence of two goals.

GOAL 1: AIM TO MAKE CYCLE TIME EQUAL TO PROCESSING TIME

The task here is to eliminate the delays and nonessential activities so that cycle time and processing time, as defined in Figure 5-2, become the same. This goal will drive not only manufacturing but also the support functions such as marketing, accounting, engineering, and purchasing to eliminate the nonessential activities that impede flow in their areas. In engineering terms, the goal is to reach *entitlement*, which is the cycle time that can be achieved with the present resources.

At KeepRite, the overall entitlement target was a reduction of cycle time from 22 days to 7 days, to be achieved over 5 years. Since entitlement was reached in about 15 months, it would have been easy to stop at that point and look for another project. Instead, the company moved to a second goal. The second goal in the sequence ensures continuous cycle time reduction.

GOAL 2: AIM FOR ZERO CYCLE TIME

A zero-based goal is obviously unattainable. However, it helps prevent people from seeing the process as a quick fix — or just another management "flavor of the month." To set a realistic operating target, research your industry and determine the lowest cycle time. This becomes the company *benchmark*, which is the best competitive level that can be achieved with added resources or capital. Although this target is likely to continuously shrink, it does represent a practical intermediate goal. It will help you determine the speed at which you have to reduce cycle time and the resources you will need to reach that level of performance.

For example, Alex Taylor noted in 1990 that Toyota's best plant requires 13 work-hours to build a vehicle as opposed to 19 to 22 work-hours per vehicle for its competitors, Nissan and Honda. He also noted that Ford performs about as well as Nissan and Honda, and did not even list Chrysler or GM.[1] When the cycle times are compared it becomes obvious that Toyota provides its competitors with a target. So, what can Toyota use as a target to encourage its own employees to reduce the 13 days even further? As the industry leader, it must shift its thinking from *benchmark* to *zero cycle time*. To move toward a zero-based goal, you must reduce processing time. To achieve the next target, you must invest capital to eliminate even more nonessentials and begin streamlining the essential activities with new technology.

The issue is not *whether* technology has a role in a CTM plant, but *when* it should be used and how much it will further reduce cycle time relative to its cost.

COMPUTER-INTEGRATED MANUFACTURING AND CTM

Computer-integrated manufacturing (CIM) represents the ultimate solution because it is the only way to reduce processing time. However, implementation is much easier and less costly if you eliminate all the nonessentials beforehand. The simplified systems will be easier to program, more effective, and less expensive. Too many companies have tried to overtake their competition by investing heavily in robots and other programmable machines that would become part of their CIM network. They discovered that jumping into CIM without first streamlining the process produces costly failures. GM, after investing more than $50 billion dollars in new technology, continues to lose market share, and its productivity remains far below its North American competitors. Sadly, even small companies that can ill afford the experiment have taken a similar course. One such company bought a $700,000 programmable punch press that seemed to make sense in its traditional batch operation. In its new plant process, however, it has become an albatross, because its output is too great for its role as part of a process.

MRP AND MRPII SYSTEMS AND CTM

Companies with MRPII systems find that their investment in the planning and procurement segments of MRPII becomes even more valuable in the new process, however, they also discover that they no longer need shop-floor controls. Further, managers will discover that the discipline required to implement and operate an effective MRPII system is valuable in the CTM transition.

If you do not have an MRPII system now you should wait until you have eliminated some of the more obvious waste before embarking on this track. KeepRite employees Kit Staley and Penny Pickering point out that the errors and sheer volume of input required by the MRP system before cycle time reduction created problems rather than solved them.

THE ROLE OF TRADITIONAL
PERFORMANCE MEASURES IN CTM

Cycle time does not replace return-on-investment measures such as the balance sheet and profit and loss; nor does it replace cash flow statements. These remain essential. However, in a CTM plant, the manager is concerned only with the output of the total process and the time that it takes to produce that output. Seen from that perspective, the traditional plant operating measures that encourage segmentation are irrelevant. For example, utilization and yield records for individual machines are no longer useful. Lead time, as we have shown, encourages buffers and discourages productivity improvement. When true flow has been achieved and cycle times are down to a few days or hours, then on-time performance is a given and does not need to be tracked. Similarly, when material inventories are delivered just in time, when manufacturing cycle time is minimal, and when the finished product spends little or no time in the warehouse, tracking inventory turns is no longer necessary.

MANUFACTURING INDUSTRIES THAT HAVE REDUCED CYCLE TIME

Manufacturing companies in many industries have ample room for improvement in cycle time (see Table 5-1). Even process manufacturers that already have a physical flow process in place can reduce cycle time. Furthermore, CTM will reveal to these

Industry	No. of Steps	No. of Value-Added Steps (Essential)	Percentage
Glass (tableware)	72	6	8%
Food processing	37	4	11%
Textile (yarns, weaving)	105	11	10%
Metal (wheel cylinders)	187	13	7%
Electronics (cable assembly)	239	19	8%
Consumer Products (disposable razors)	105	10	10%

Table 5-1. Analysis of Activities in Several Industries

companies that support services such as order entry are another source of nonessential activities. In fact, it will show that 60 to 65 percent of the cycle time is absorbed before any value-adding or essential manufacturing steps are performed. The trick is to empower employees to expose and eliminate nonessential activities in an organized way.

CYCLE TIME MEASUREMENT TECHNIQUES

Many senior managers are skeptical about the dramatic savings that can result from cycle time reductions. To convince them, we provide the following method for establishing the baseline cycle time.

Establishing Baseline Cycle Time

There are seven steps in establishing baseline:

1. Determine the scope.
2. Assign an interdisciplinary team.
3. Identify each element within the loop or process.
4. Characterize the process elements.
5. Develop flow diagrams.
6. Measure actual times for each element of the process.
7. Sum individual times.

Step 1: Define the scope of the project. This can be the scope of a total business or a segment of the business. If the scope is the total business, it may be the make/market loop or the design/development loop. Typically baseline is established for a measurable unit within a major loop.

Step 2: Assign an interdisciplinary team to measure the cycle or process. (If the cycle time reduction project is localized in one discipline, one or two people may be appropriate.) The teams should be composed of representatives of each major subsystem involved in the loop or process. It is usually necessary to get feedback from people directly involved in each subsystem to verify and validate the data.

Step 3: Define each element or activity for the loop or process. In manufacturing environments the various elements of a process are usually well understood and documented. In direct or support organizations, however, this is often not the case and a cross-functional team of people may be required to identify all elements of the process.

Step 4: Characterize each of the subelements of the loop or process. This involves understanding the *inputs* such as people's skills, equipment, and the measurement system; *process* such as type of work done, methods used, and sequence of activities; *outputs* such as the product or feedback to other subelements; and organization *interfaces* and interrelationships.

In preparation for calculating the cycle time of each subelement, identify the number of units started and completed in each subelement for a given time period as well as the number of activities in process and/or inventory at the beginning and end of the given time period.

One pitfall of this step is listing in detail all inputs, outputs, and process elements rather than focusing on the critical ones. Another pitfall is collecting massive amounts of information that you are not sure you will use.

Step 5: Develop flow diagrams. Routing is usually better documented in manufacturing environments where extensive questioning may be necessary to piece together a routing. For each subelement, the questions should be similar in content and purpose, but should generally be phrased to reflect the specific subelement being diagrammed.

The series of questions should follow a "What happens next?" format. The answer to each question is recorded, and further questioning continues until the entire process is documented. It is often necessary to probe "if...then" situations to document various branches in activities that occur. The main flow of a product or information may follow one path, while special cases may be redirected to an alternate path. It is essential that the special routing be investigated and documented since the cycle times for the special routes often are significantly different from those for the regular routing through subelements. During this step many barriers to short cycle time may surface. "Why does it take so long?" is a good question to stimulate visibility to barriers.

It is possible, and highly probable, that the process flow will often lead to and from other subelements. Indeed, the work flow may take products or information through a single subelement multiple times. Each time the product or information backtracks through the same subelement, it should be noted since additional cycle time is being accumulated.

Step 6: Measure the actual times required for the product or information to flow through the subelements. There are two different techniques for measuring the actual times. They are:

- use of a formula
- use of "lot travelers" or dated documents

Use of the formulas to calculate baseline cycle time will provide an average cycle time. The formulas can be based on actions in process, input and output rates, or on output rate only, depending on the particular application. The advantage of formula calculations is that the cycle times can be computed on the basis of data that are either already available or easily accessible. The disadvantage is that the calculations do not reveal where in the process delays are occurring or why; nor does it provide any distribution data regarding the frequency of occurrence versus cycle time.

Formulas. The formula for *calculating baseline cycle time* is *actions in process* divided by *processing speed*. Note that these data were collected in Step 4.

The formula for production cycle time is depicted as

$$CT = \frac{\text{Average actions in process}}{\text{Average speed of line *}}$$

$$\text{Average speed of line} = \frac{\text{Start rate + Out rate}}{2}$$

---

* Actions processed per period of time

Where a yield loss occurs, the speed of the line can be defined as the output rate divided by the yield plus half the yield loss expressed as a decimal fraction. For example, if the output rate is 1,000 per day and the yield is 80 percent (yield loss 20 percent), then the speed of the line is $1,000/(.80 + .20/2) = 1,000/.9 = 1,111.11$ per day.

Note that if the measurement is actions processed per day then the resulting cycle time is expressed in days.

Consider the following formula for *calculating manufacturing cycle time* for printed circuit board assemblies (one activity in a process).

Printed circuit board assemblies for month:

- Beginning board inventory   4,600
- Ending board inventory   3,600
- Boards to stock: 32,000
- Boards started in line: 31,000

$$CT = \frac{\text{Average work in process}}{\text{Speed of line}} = \frac{\frac{\text{Beg. inv.} + \text{End inv.}}{2}}{\frac{\text{Start rate} + \text{Out rate}}{2}}$$

$$= \frac{\frac{(4,600 + 3,600)}{2}}{\frac{32,000 + 31,000}{2}} = \frac{4,100}{31,500} \text{ months}$$

$$= .13 \ (21 \text{ days/month}) = 2.7 \text{ days}$$

This tells you that an average board requires 2.7 working days to progress through the line. It does not give the distribution (fastest, slowest, etc.).

The formula for *calculating service cycle time* is depicted as:

$$CT = \frac{\text{Actions in process}}{\text{Actions completed per time period}}$$

Consider the following formula for *calculating order-entry cycle time.*

Order-entry activity for month (sales orders received to one backlog):

		Totals	
		Right	Wrong
• Beginning orders in process		400	300
– On hold—price	50		
– On hold—engineering	50		
– Released to system	300		
• Ending orders in process		500	300
– On hold—price	100		
– On hold—engineering	100		
– Released to system	300		
• Orders completed during month		450	
• Orders started during month		550	

Right	Wrong
$$CT = \frac{\text{Actions in process}}{\text{Actions/time period}}$$	$$CT = \frac{\text{Actions in process}}{\text{Actions/time period}}$$
$$CT = \frac{\frac{(400 + 500)}{2}}{\frac{(400 + 500)}{2}} = \frac{450}{550}$$	$$CT = \frac{\frac{(300 + 300)}{2}}{\frac{(450 + 550)}{2}} = \frac{300}{500}$$
= 0.90 mos. (21 days/mo.)	= 0.60 mos. (21 days/mo.)
= 18.9 days	= 12.6 days

Note that work-in-process on hold for any reason should be included, since the real cycle time, as perceived by the customer, includes on-hold items. The causes for on-hold often highlight barriers to short cycle time.

Lot travelers. Use of "lot travelers" is an alternative method of calculating cycle time. Any dated record that shows the start dates, intermediate position dates, and finish dates can be used as the equivalent of a lot traveler. Lot travelers are commonly used in manufacturing.

NOTE

1. Alex Taylor III, "Why Toyota Keeps Getting Better and Better and Better," *Fortune,* 19 November 1990, p. 72.

6

Employees:
The Drivers of Fast-Track CTM

Because they treat each machine as a discrete unit whose efficiency must be measured, traditional shop-floor operators have become button-pushers. In a CTM plant, by contrast, if one machine is down, all are considered to be down. This view encourages operators to work as a team. Further, in a fast-track CTM transition, managers must be prepared to give employees more power to run their own work area. This means delegating to them many of the functions currently done by supervisory personnel. Since nonessential activities are buried in every traditional job, the cycle time reduction process provides everyone with opportunities to gain a sense of achievement and recognition.

Participative management does not mean that senior management can delegate the leadership role. On the contrary, a successful transition to CTM requires strong and committed senior management leadership.

In a traditional manufacturing process, managers aim to ensure that the WIP moves from station to station in a way that keeps machine utilization high. All they expect from operators and clerical people is *consistent output* from their individual workstations. In this operating environment there is no need for teamwork — no need for individual operators to be anything more than button-pushers. "Leave your brains at the door and pick them up when you leave" is a commonly heard phrase that symbolizes the traditional operator's job. People work independently taking input, performing the job, and adding the completed unit to the queue on the other side. For example, process engineers work independently of design engineers and both work independently of the shop floor. The sequence of activities from order to shipment could best be described as "each department throwing the problems over the wall to the next group." As a result, the shop-floor workers inevitably have to do their best with what they get. Defects are an accepted and even expected part of the process. Assembly is expected to find a piece that will fit or can be made to fit.

The traditional operating style promotes attitudes that stifle initiative — the "we've always done it this way" and "mind your own business" attitudes are particularly common. A frightening example of this attitude occurred in a Canadian plant that works with toxic chemicals. A delivery truck caught fire at the receiving dock. The staff was well trained and was able to put the fire out before the city fire department arrived. If the fire had burned for a few more minutes it would have created a toxic cloud over a fairly large city. Senior management investigated the accident and found that most of the employees had known all along that the way the trucks were unloaded could cause a fire. In fact, they had been waiting for the inevitable accident. When individuals were asked why they had not brought their concerns forward, the clear answer was "We did, and we were told by the supervisor to 'mind your own business.' " Even though this accident could have had catastrophic results, the supervisor held fast to the traditional operating style.

THE EMPLOYEE'S NEW ROLES

In the CTM operation, everyone is part of a team and all functions are interdependent. Job activities differ dramatically from those of traditional operations. Compare the tasks of traditional operators with those of CTM operators (see Table 6-1).[1]

Does the first list of employee activities look familiar? For too many companies, unfortunately, the answer is yes. In a CTM plant, however, where all nonessential activities have been eliminated,

Traditional Job	CTM Job
Plan Recreational activities Collective bargaining Moonlighting opportunities "Escape" activities Reading "help-wanted" ads Retirement options Job security issues Vacations and holidays	**Plan** Production requirements Balance kanban system Tool and equipment layout Maintenance schedules Work sampling procedures Idle time utilization Fishbone and Pareto charts
Do Monitor work rule compliance Hassle high achievers Pay and benefit comparisons Call attention to inequities Evaluate safety practices Check time-keeping accuracy Follow up management promises	**Do** Record production data Operate equipment Lubricate equipment Adjust equipment Arrange workplace Maintain tidy work areas Activate signal lights Post production data
Control File grievances Follow instructions Operate equipment Report equipment malfunctions Keep production line going Keep busy (or look busy) Attend safety meetings Horseplay and other diversions	**Control** Evaluate production data Diagnose quality problems Check machine performance Stop and start production Evaluate tool layout Review customer feedback Adjust equipment Request staff assistance

Source: Adapted from M. Scott Myers, "Don't Let JIT Become a North American Quick Fix," *Business Quarterly,* 51 (4 March 1987): 33 (Exhibit 6) and 34 (Exhibit 7). Reprinted by permission of Business Quarterly, published by the Western Business School, The University of Western Ontario, London, Ontario, Canada.

Table 6-1. Traditional versus CTM Job Tasks

everyone is involved and operators take on some responsibilities that in traditional plants are restricted to supervisors.

Thus in a CTM company, the operator's status rises. The rationale is simple. Only the person doing the job knows where the nonessential activities in that job are located. Moreover, the same person can insure that those nonessential activities remain buried. Therefore, to obtain positive employee involvement, the company must invest in training that shows employees how to work in teams. Outside consultants cannot change the organizational culture or improve productivity as dramatically as properly trained employees. Outsiders can "cherry-pick" what seems to the uninitiated to be dramatic productivity improvement in specific areas, but only employees working in teams that are part of a management culture can continuously improve the total company process.

Perhaps the greatest testimony to that statement exists in the experience of Toyota and General Motors. Since 1980 GM has invested $50 billion in CIM.[2] In 1987, GM reported 20 to 40 percent productivity gains at plants that use team-based manufacturing systems.[3] Its joint venture with Toyota (New United Motor Manufacturing, Inc. or NUMMI) was soon among the most productive plants in GM, even though the technology was old and inferior. Throughout the 1980s, there were many productivity improvement projects going on across the organization. None of them had much impact on the organization as a whole, however. As of 1990, GM required 766,000 people to make 8 million vehicles,[4] compared with Toyota's requirement of 91, 790 people to make 4.4 million vehicles. Worse, GM's average vehicle cycle time was more than 22 hours,[5] compared with Toyota's cycle time of just 13 hours.

You might think that all that GM has to do is aim to reach 13 hours at some predetermined time in the future. The problem is that the teams running Toyota's operations are continuously reducing cycle time. Therefore, that low target is constantly moving lower.

Teams are an essential part of the evolution to CTM (see Chapter 8). Three types of teams are necessary to integrate the disparate units into a single operating process. The first task is to establish *cross-functional review teams* of key employees. The job of these teams is to describe the cycle time reduction opportunities across the entire company process. When the opportunities have been developed into projects, senior management ranks them according to priority and then assigns them to *project teams*, which work on eliminating impediments to cycle time reduction in their areas.

Members of the review teams form the nucleus of each project team. This is the point where the expertise and experience of the operators and clerical workers is introduced. Initially, there may be 10 to 15 project teams, but there will probably be at least 150 to 200 documented opportunities or projects to be completed. As projects are completed, others are established and more employees become involved. Eventually, most employees will work on a project team.

Many operators and clerical workers begin the cycle time reduction process with an awareness of the nonessential components of their job. As members of project teams, they helped to eliminate them. As a result of this experience, they may already be deeply involved in running the day-to-day operating process as members of supervised work teams. It will be a corporate decision whether they are encouraged to form *self-directed work teams* that take on the supervisory functions of planning their daily work, organizing themselves, and staffing the team.

Some readers may doubt the capability or interest of their employees in making such contributions. The experiences of companies that did involve employees in seeking productivity improvement ideas should allay their qualms.

Consider Ford's experience in a plant about to be converted for the building of a new model — the Taurus. As Robert Waterman reports, Ford benefited in two ways when it sent engineers out to get suggestions from shop-floor operators.

Imaginative cost-saving suggestions. The engineers accumulated 1,401 ideas from the line operators. They were able to incorporate about 700 of the suggestions with clear economic benefits. For example, one simple suggestion was to replace the practice of two people hanging the dashboards with the use of a locater pin placed in one corner. The pin ensured a perfect setting and allowed one operator to fasten both sides.

Another operator suggested a one-piece body side and doors, "so we have integrity in the door margins and a better overall fit." The engineers were unable to acquire a press large enough to accomplish this aim, but they did get the design down to a 2-piece assembly, from the previous design of 12 or 15 pieces.[6]

Improved morale and employee commitment. The employees whose ideas were incorporated were obviously pleased. Those whose suggestions were not accepted were told why. In this way they too had been recognized: their ideas had been considered, even if not ultimately adopted. Even skeptical or hesitant employees will catch the spirit when they see how others' suggestions are handled.

To "own" an innovation is generally accepted as the first step to implementing it. If 1,401 employee suggestions were recognized in developing the process, who owns the Taurus? Everybody!

Does it make a difference who owns the car? Of course, because operator ownership gives internal meaning to the company motto "Quality is Job 1." If all the operators feel involved, then personal pride will seep into their daily jobs. As the Taurus moved into production, Ford was progressing toward a more dynamic and motivating work environment. The button-pusher operator was replaced by a more motivated creative thinker.

Other companies have also benefited significantly from employee contributions:

- General Electric's Erie, Pennsylvania plant was producing a complicated door that required sophisticated tooling. As a result of the shop workers' suggestions, the door is now built with simple tooling, using 40 percent fewer parts and costing 25 to 30 percent less to make.[7]
- At Budd Manufacturing's plant in Kitchener, Ontario, a team was able to reduce rework on their stampings line from around 35 to 8 percent. Assembly has reduced defects from 20 to 8 percent.[8]
- At NBC (a GE subsidiary) work teams "scotched forms that totaled more than 2 million pieces of paper." [9]

Engineers and managers at GE and Budd could not have made such impacts on productivity without the help of knowledgeable people on the shop floor.

However, a potential danger lurks in adopting the participative approach. If the process is treated as an isolated project and dies when the change is completed, then the upbeat atmosphere will quickly evaporate. Honda of America avoided this danger by institutionalizing the suggestion concept through its voluntary improvement program (VIP). In 1989, 85 percent of the workers in its motorcycle plant were involved in a VIP project. In a CTM plant, the continuous cycle time reduction goal ensures that the positive atmosphere can be continuous.

EMPOWERING EMPLOYEES IN CTM

Before you embark on a fast-track CTM evolution, you must be prepared to broaden the decision-making process and give employee work teams more power to run their own work areas. To adopt this approach with confidence, you have to believe your people have the ability to make the difference.

You may already have some evidence of the impact that employees working in teams can have on productivity. If not, the following story will give you some insight. Here a new manager attempted to replace a work-team with a more traditional system. Although the story makes no mention of essential versus nonessential activities or costs, it requires little imagination to visualize the buildup of nonessential activities and their costs in Phase 2 of this company's evolution.

The story is told by Gordon Holland, a production worker with SOS, Inc., in Midland, Texas.[10]

This single-product electronics company consisted of 20 employees. It was small and cohesive when taken over by a division of Hughes Tool. After the takeover, it was moved from its garage to a small plant, but the work group remained a naturally cohesive team. Production workers, engineers, managers, and salespeople all had easy access to one another on the informal shop floor. As time went on, Holland and his colleagues learned and mastered more and more of the tasks required to make the product. As result, Holland felt a deep sense of ownership over the finished product.

Then the operation was moved to the division's home base in Oklahoma. Holland moved with it, but many people did not go. Phase 2 started after the move, when division executives started to "modernize" the operation. They set up the research and development function in a separate building next door. Then they segmented the production work and assigned individual workers to small parts of the total process. Later, they created separate departments for human resources, order processing, purchasing, testing, quality control, maintenance, accounting, and marketing, with most headed by division people. Holland's job was limited to troubleshooting the many delays and quality problems that began cropping up. In a brief 18 months after the operation had been reorganized, the highly integrated and effective work team had become a dysfunctional bureaucracy. In Holland's words, "We were a mess. And nobody seemed to notice that good people didn't get involved anymore."

Phase 3 began when Senior Vice President Clint Boyd took charge. After many discussions with Holland and others, he decided to increase worker involvement and revamp support functions using self-directed teams. These teams went on to reintegrate the work force and catapult productivity far beyond its level in the SOS garage. As Holland observes, "It's not just a matter of turning people loose to go back to the good old days. It's a planned process for giving responsibility to the people who know what to do at their level and when to get other people involved."

This story reflects the experiences of many work teams in the United States. SOS started as a naturally integrated team. When it "modernized" (or adopted the traditional approach, as we call it in this book), it installed specialists and narrow job categories that destroyed the flexibility and commitment that made the company a desirable acquisition in the first place.

As Hughes found out, self-directed teams resurrected an aspect of the past — the personal satisfaction employees derive from making broad contributions to a small-scale enterprise — that can quicken the pulse of many companies prepared to take the necessary steps.

Our experience suggests that individuals working in the process every day understand the subtleties of their respective jobs. If you allow them to discover the requirements of the total process, they will at the least identify the nonessential activities that only they know are buried there. Many of them will also play significant roles in eliminating these activities.

It is important to discover the latent talents of your people. One way to do so is to ask how many have fix-it skills. At a minimum, most will have had to work with a car mechanic or appliance technician in diagnosing problems. Some may have done minor repairs or maintenance on their own cars or appliances. You may even find people with trades from other countries who didn't feel comfortable enough with the language to take the exams. As a result, their special abilities remain unrecognized and unused. Many skills that tend to be ignored in a traditional process can be put to good use in a CTM process.

If you expect employees to contribute suggestions for productivity improvement you must be prepared to act on them. You cannot defer decisions on them and still expect the group to maintain its momentum. *Remember, a negative response is acceptable as long as you provide valid reasons.*

You must also share recognition for improvements. Consider yourself a collaborator, rather than sitting in judgment on individual success or failure.

You may protest that employee involvement creates a long and cumbersome process. It's true that the information-gathering and planning stages may appear to cause delays. Implementation time will be greatly reduced, however, because the group will know what has to be done. And since they were part of the planning, they will be prepared to do it. As well, when a few small successes appear, other people will want to join the team and the momentum for change will accelerate.

INVESTING IN STAFF DEVELOPMENT

Traditional companies seldom have staff development programs. After all, if people are operating independently, they need little more than basic training on the machine or in processing the paper. This sort of informal training is traditionally done by the outgoing incumbent or the immediate supervisor.

With CTM, staff development is a vital part of transforming cost centers and button-pushers into a team dedicated to continuous improvement. A formal education program is needed for two reasons:

1. To the uninitiated, CTM is like a foreign culture: It has a radically different way of viewing things. Employees need to have the fundamentals of the new way explained so that they understand and feel comfortable with the goals of reducing cycle time and creating a total linear business flow.
2. An education program enables employees to see where their particular jobs fit into the total operating process and to understand how the concept of interdependent jobs will make their work more interesting.

Integrated with CTM training is a cooperative planning exercise, with time on the job to accomplish the task. Fortunately, such time is easier to find in CTM, since idle time is the line-balancing buffer in a pull flow process.

Obviously, CTM staff development is more comprehensive than technical training or retraining in new technology. Ford's Bill Anderson, manager of the production and option programming department, describes how managers must perceive training: "Training . . . is moving into the strategic realm. Our goal to establish participative management supports our long-term strategy to become more efficient and productive. As employees become more efficient in organizational interrelationships and more satisfied with their jobs, they are better able to make meaningful contributions." [11]

How Much Should You Invest?

Many companies in the United States already look upon training as a capital expense, justifying these outlays in the same way as they justify investments in technology. For example, Motorola has documented savings of 30 times the dollars invested.[12] If you manage by cycle time, cost reduction will be considerable — and measurable.

If your company employs 200 to 300 people, you can get a very good program for everyone for an investment of $75,000 to $100,000, not including the cost of the time away from the job. The returns come from reducing WIP and cycle time. There is mounting evidence that an investment in staff development produces greater returns than a similar investment in equipment.

Japanese carmakers are leading proponents of training as an investment. Toyota's plant in Cambridge, Ontario, proves the point. The capital cost of the new plant was $450 million. The pre-start-up training budget was $40 million. Shop-floor workers were hired and before the plant opened were given four months of training in Cambridge; some went to Japan for more training. As a result, Toyota's usual start-up performance requirements were not only met but in many cases exceeded. Toyota executives believe that

- an untrained work force is a great obstacle to a successful start-up
- local people can be hired and developed to achieve or even better the Toyota performance requirements

If you are still skeptical, consider the alternatives.

Alternatives to Investment in Training

Some managers may think that they can *buy machines and eliminate people*. GM executives thought this way until they entered into a joint venture with Toyota (NUMMI) that changed their minds. Although NUMMI uses out-of-date technology to assemble Chevy Novas, its productivity is higher than most of GM's new high-technology plants. The key is Toyota's management style, which emphasizes thorough training, participative management, lean layers of middle management, and decision making that is pushed as close as possible to the assembly line.[13]

As a result of the Toyota experience, GM has stopped thinking of technology as instant salvation and is now heavily involved in programs to retrain and cross-train employees.

There are other ways of circumventing the training requirement. For example, some managers may choose to lay off their present work force and instead *hire already trained people*. These managers should read the results of a recent study by GTE Communications Systems. They indicate that it is cheaper to retrain existing employees than to hire and integrate new skilled people.[14]

Still, many managers remain unconvinced that any major training program is required. For example, a recent survey revealed that 73 percent of firms in Ontario, Canada's industrial heartland, have no formal training programs. Where firms do offer training, only a small proportion of employees are included. However, the same study showed that the companies that did invest in training were the industry leaders.[15]

Competitive pressures have pushed the automotive industry to invest in staff development. Soon they will push other industries to do the same.

MANAGER ROLES IN A CTM OPERATION

Participative management is essential to fast-track CTM. In the words of General Electric's CEO Jack Welch, "We've got to take out the boss element." [16] The process requires leaders who set the direction but are willing to acknowledge that employees working in teams are vital to the evolution of CTM. In some CTM plants, teams of empowered employees run the day-to-day operations. CTM managers need not worry that their own status will be diminished in these new operating patterns. If they encourage employees to take more responsibility they will soon discover that their position is enhanced. Furthermore, as a result of the superior information produced by the teams, managers will discover that the decisions they are still expected to make are better. An account of two incidents at GE's Canadian operation perhaps best explains the manager's new decision-making role.

At a plant in Bromont, Quebec, a team of employees proposed that rather than waiting for an authorizing signature, the operators should be empowered to spend up to $500 to get a die or tool fixed. The manager accepted the suggestion immediately, whereupon he received a five-minute round of applause. Did that manager lose status?

In an accounts receivable department in another CGE division, the clerks handling collections suggested that they be given the authority to negotiate settlements immediately for all accounts under $2,000 without recourse to their manager. They were able to show that the vast majority of their overdue accounts were due to a customer looking for redress. The clerks' rationale was that they thought it was better to sort out the problem quickly rather than have a customer angry for months. Management bought the idea and raised the amount from $2,000 to $5,000. Was the managers' status diminished? Was this decision too important to forgo? In the CTM environment, the managers' job is not to command and control but to coordinate by removing impediments and improving communications.

Team Building

Teams require leaders. A CTM team leader requires two attributes. First is the ability to chair a meeting and run a project. Second and most important is the ability to command respect from the team members. A leader can be assigned by a senior manager, but the team will be more effective if it is led by its natural leader. The natural leader knows how to handle his or her team members.

Even in a traditional plant, where an autocratic management style dominates the formal structure, there are informal leaders who operate in parallel. They can speak and act on behalf of their colleagues in discussions with both management and union. These informal leaders may themselves be good team leaders or they may be able to suggest suitable candidates. In any event, you should consult them when introducing CTM and specifically when you are looking for team leaders. It should be noted that even with a good leader, to build a successful team requires several conditions:

1. *A common goal:* CTM goals encourage all to make continuous cycle time reduction efforts.
2. *A common language:* As stated elsewhere in the book, CTM has its own language — special terminology, practices, performance measures, and a unique set of assumptions about how to operate a business. Since employees must be able to work effectively as one team in CTM, all employees must understand the language of CTM.
3. *An understanding of the dual roles of each employee:* The employees' first responsibility in both a traditional and a CTM plant is to keep the day-to-day process operating effectively. In a CTM plant, however, they are also given responsibility for exposing and eliminating nonessential activities.

4. *Cooperation:* All tasks in the CTM process are interdependent. Therefore, one of the manager's most important functions is to eliminate impediments. Lack of authority to decide is a major impediment to a team's success. As we saw above, the operators and collection clerks were impeded by a lack of authority to make decisions that were seemingly small but critical to their ability to perform.

On the other hand, employees do expect managers to make the key decisions. The decision process in a transition to CTM would be structured as follows:

1. Set the goal (management's role).
2. Gather information and develop ideas (employees' role).
3. Create the evolution plan (employees create the plan, management approves it).
4. Implement the plan (employees' role).
5. Evaluate the changes (management's role).

Just as managers expect certain things from employees, so do employees expect certain things from managers. Ask any group of employees what they expect from their leader and the same thoughts will surface every time. They want a boss who is honest, competent, and able to create an environment that motivates. To be effective as a leader in CTM you must demonstrate these characteristics.

Honesty

The honest boss is usually the respected boss. In the context of CTM, *honesty* assumes that:

- if a promise is made, it will be kept
- if support is given it will not be withdrawn at the first sign of trouble
- if decisions are required, they will be made and will be unequivocal
- "cover your tracks" memos are unnecessary

In a CTM transition you must deliver on promises — whether the thing promised is an authorization, money for a capital purchase, or a raise for a team member. A failure to deliver on promises breeds distrust. If team members trust their manager, they will get on with managing the change.

Competence

Managers will be judged on their ability to provide a plausible direction and to react positively under pressure. Technical competence is secondary to managerial competence. This explains why more and more companies are promoting employees who have people skills rather than exclusively technical skills.

As a manager you can actually capitalize on a lack of technical knowledge to enlist assistance skills from others and thus convert a personal deficiency into a team builder.

Motivation

Managers must be enthusiastic, positive, and energetic. They have to make a strong public commitment to the project. But to motivate others, they must also get them to buy into company goals and accept them as their own. They must create an environment that will motivate people.

Herzberg suggests that four actions will foster this motivation: [17]

1. *Encourage participation.* Get input from every level.
2. *Foster achievement.* Most people are exhilarated when they achieve an objective. A challenge overcome provides them with an emotional "high."
3. *Show appreciation even for rejected ideas.* Often simple congratulations, or some form of public recognition are sufficient. In the Taurus project, Ford was effective in handling those employee suggestions that they did not accept. They recognized each effort with thanks and a personal communication as to why the idea would not work under the specific circumstances of the moment.

   Managers can also use Blanchard and Johnson's notion of "catching people doing things right" and giving a "one-minute praising" to personalize their communication and build enthusiasm.[18] Daily recognition of concrete achievement and contribution drives the continuous improvement process and creates a motivating environment. Cheerleading without specific recognition of actual jobs well done soon sounds hollow. Willingness to share the limelight is what makes you a motivator.

As cycle time decreases, employees will want to share in the benefits. It is doubtful that across-the-board pay increases, awarded to all regardless of effort or contribution, motivate anybody. Piecework compensation, such as commissions, is generally perceived as a motivator, but because it rewards operators for *individual* effort, it is incompatible with CTM. By contrast, gain sharing rewards *group* performance and thus encourages team effort. This type of motivator is gaining popularity.

4. *Give employees a chance to grow.* Most people want opportunities to advance, take on more challenging work, or acquire greater responsibility. In the CTM process, such opportunities exist everywhere: the opportunities to train and chair action teams are but two examples. At one company, an employee must have chaired an action team before being considered for a supervisor's job.

Herzberg argues that managers should build motivators into jobs as part of a "job enrichment" program. Those who tried to implement his ideas ran into problems, however. The lack of a process that demanded teamwork coupled with the lack of a simple performance measure made it difficult to embed the job enrichment concept into the organizational culture. In a CTM company, the ability to measure the impact of each change on cycle time will provide the necessary sense of achievement for both the individual and the group. CTM is designed to embed a continuous cycle time reduction process into the corporate culture.

Handling Potential Layoffs

Recently, management analysts have added *job security* to Herzberg's list of motivators. In this context job security is based not on seniority but on ability. When a company has invested time and money in training its employees and seen returns from that investment, it only makes sense to retain those employees. Indeed, job security will not be an issue in companies adopting CTM in an expanding market. In a diminishing market or overstaffed company, however, you may not be able to guarantee job security.

In such situations you must consider several issues:

- How many of the core people would survive a layoff on the basis of the present seniority clause?
- What provisions would have to be made if the criterion for retention was switched from seniority to contribution?
- What other avenues are open to provide an orderly reduction of staff, such as early retirement or normal attrition?
- Is it preferable to make one major cut or let the numbers go down over time?

There are no hard and fast rules to laying off employees. However, these guidelines may help you reduce staff without lowering morale:

- If possible, use attrition rather than layoffs to reduce the complement.
- If overstaffed, downsize before getting into staff development.
- Analyze future skill needs carefully to ensure that after the downsizing the remaining group has the talent to help in the transition.

One of our clients, seeing the implications of CTM, spent an entire year downsizing the operation before doing any further training. As a result, when the time came to invest in the people that were left, he was able to put all his remaining people through the development programs so that everyone understood the CTM practices and performance measures. More important, he was able to let them know that they were the key to the CTM transition and, therefore, to the company's future.

KeepRite took a different approach to staff reduction. The company was in the middle of its cycle time reduction process when forced to lay off about 40 percent of its work force. To those who were laid off, however, it showed its appreciation in an unusual way. In response to a union request, the company delayed the layoff date by two days to give the employees more money and less waiting time for unemployment insurance. Don Kivell tells what the company did: "We put them on training for two days. As a result, people walked out feeling wanted and we had increased their skill level."

First-line supervisors need special consideration. Inevitably, some managers and supervisors will have to be dismissed because they are unable to move from an autocratic to a participative management style, even with training and education. The first-line supervisors will be especially burdened after such layoffs since fewer of them will have to take on greater responsibility. They will suddenly have to oversee whole processes rather than specific functions. They will be managing more people and be responsible for functions that they may not be experts in. In other words, they will have to trust the experts who work for them and delegate many responsibilities traditionally entrusted to supervisors to these experts. They will have to spend more time planning and implementing change — two functions some of them will not be comfortable with. However, if handled with patience and care, some of these people will make excellent trainers and be happy to move into the jobs that open up during transition. For those who are unable to adjust, you will have to devise equitable ways of easing them out or moving them into other jobs.

NOTES

1. M. Scott Myers, "Don't Let JIT Become a North American Quick Fix," *Business Quarterly,* 51:4 (March 1987), p. 33 (Exhibit 6) and p. 34 (Exhibit 7).
2. Taylor, "Why Toyota Keeps Getting Better and Better and Better," *Fortune,* 19 November 1990, pp. 68 and 72.
3. Ibid.
4. Ibid.
5. Ibid.
6. Robert H. Waterman, *The Renewal Factor* (New York: Bantam Books, 1987), pp. 82-85.
7. Otis Port and John W. Wilson, "Making Brawn Work with Brains," *Business Week,* 20 April 1987, p. 58.
8. Herbert Wedderburn, "JIT as a Survival Strategy," *Industrial Management,* July 1985, p. 14.
9. Thomas A. Stewart, "GE Keeps Those Ideas Coming," *Fortune,* 12 August 1991, p. 44.
10. Jack D. Orsburn, et al., *Self-Directed Work Teams: The New American Challenge* (Homewood, Ill.: Business One Irwin, 1990), p. 6.
11. Derwin A. Fox and Alfred M. Tarquinio, "The Strategic Business Approach to Training," *National Productivity Review,* Summer 1987, p. 270.
12. Michael Brody, "Helping Workers Work Smarter," *Fortune,* 8 June 1987, p. 87.
13. Russell Mitchell, "Detroit Stumbles on Its Way to the Future," *Business Week,* 16 June 1986, pp. 103-4.
14. Bill Sorporito, "Cutting Costs without Cutting People: A Study of Work in America," *Fortune,* 27 May 1987, p. 30.
15. Ontario Ministry of Skills Development, *Ontario's Training Strategy,* September 1986, p. 7.
16. Stewart, "GE Keeps Those Ideas Coming," p. 41.
17. Frederick Herzberg, "One More Time: How Do You Motivate Employees?" *Harvard Business Review,* September-October 1987, pp. 112-13.
18. Kenneth Blanchard and Spencer Johnson, *The One Minute Manager* (New York: Berkley Books, 1983).

7

Impact of Cycle Time Reduction on Profits

OVERVIEW

In previous chapters we have dealt with the goal of entitlement — the cycle time that can be achieved simply through elimination of nonessential activities across the company. We outlined a cycle time reduction sequence that begins with the elimination of nonessential activities and impediments to linear flow in the manufacturing cycle. We showed that as nonessentials are eliminated, buffer inventories can be reduced dramatically.

In this chapter we show how reaching entitlement affects not only profits but also most of the functions and responsibilities of the chief financial officer (CFO). Traditionally, CFOs have avoided getting involved in cycle time reduction, but in the fast-track process their involvement is essential. Once involved, they will realize that continuous cycle time reduction

- improves profits dramatically
- improves the balance sheet
- reduces the working capital cycle
- introduces new asset-valuation criteria
- simplifies internal controls
- requires a new cost model

IMPROVEMENT OF PROFITS

Eliminating nonessential activities such as changeovers and travel time may not reduce costs. As suggested in Chapter 4, however, it may reduce inventories and their many associated costs. Included in the associated costs are the cost of those jobs necessary to buffer nonessential activities, such as expediting, cycle counting, and shepherding engineering changes.

KeepRite Canada's performance provides an example of how a significant drop in cycle time produces a similar reduction in inventories. Recall that in the first year employees reduced cycle time from 22 days to 7 days and inventories from $18 million to $3 million. As KeepRite's profit and loss statement shows, the ripple effect of such a major inventory drop extends across a large spectrum of expense accounts. Some examples follow.

Interest charges. As inventories diminish, loans (and corresponding interest charges) are reduced.

Facilities expenses. The linear flow process requires much less space because there is no inventory and no travel between machines. Whether the extra space can be rented out or used for other purposes is up to the company. Often, operations in other buildings can be brought in to fill the excess space, after which the other buildings can be sublet. In any event, better use of space reduces expenses for rent, taxes, heat, light, and power.

Material handling. While forklift trucks, storage racks and bins, and pallets or containers may be needed as part of the receiving and shipping process, they will not be needed in the plant linear process.

Every forklift truck that can be eliminated reduces costs by about $60,000 per year. At KeepRite, the number of towmotors has already dropped from 33 to 22, for a savings of about $660,000 and further eliminations are expected as the company tries to keep pace with one of its Japanese competitors, which has no towmotors on its shop floor.

Administrative costs. Indirect labor costs go down when people eliminate specialized functions such as expediters and changeover teams. They also drop when internal control procedures are simplified. An obvious example is the cycle counter. As we outline later in this chapter, internal control processes can become bottlenecks in the drive to achieve total linear flow. Many of these nonessential procedures create other costs related to computer time and paper forms.

Quality improvement. As quality defects are reduced to parts per million, costs diminish in the following expense accounts:

- warranties
- obsolescence
- scrap
- rework of damaged goods

Direct labor clerical costs. Since direct labor in most operations will account for 5 to 10 percent of the total cost, it will not likely be segregated from overheads with the same degree of accuracy as a traditional cost system requires. Time tickets and separate printouts will then be redundant. At that point, all the costs of the clerical activities associated with segregating direct labor will disappear.

Organizational structural changes. Other costs will disappear as operators take control of the linear flow process, which leads to fewer management levels and job classifications. Depending on their size, companies will probably end up with two to four classifications and four to six levels of management.

Workers' compensation costs. High workers' compensation costs may drop dramatically. Most worker injuries are to the back, and are caused by moving inventory.

Expenses That Increase in CTM

Some expenses will increase during the evolution to CTM:

1. *Maintenance* will increase significantly. Whereas preventive maintenance will be done by operators, planned

maintenance (to decrease the chances for total system shutdown) will increase markedly.

2. *Education and training* expenses will increase. The amount will depend on the number of employees.
3. *Sundry small expenditures* may be required to fix tools and move equipment to reduce changeover and travel times.
4. *Revenue increases* may occur. If the company is in an expanding market, it may increase throughputs during the same accounting period, and in turn increase revenues.

Despite the expenses associated with a transition to CTM, the net increase in profits can be substantial. One of our original clients went from $2.5 million loss to a $2.5 million profit in about 18 months — "the most spectacular achievement in the company's history," said a former controller. Unfortunately, since the company treated cycle time reduction as a project rather than a way of life, its subsequent performance slipped dramatically.

IMPROVEMENT OF THE BALANCE SHEET

While most people will focus on the improved profits, they should not overlook the positive impact of significant inventory reduction on the balance sheet and working capital indicators. Remember that in the first year KeepRite Canada reduced its inventories from $18 million to $3 million.

Since no new investment in technology is required in the effort to reach entitlement, the only things likely to change are current assets and, if there is a bank loan, current liabilities. If you follow the KeepRite path, the balance sheet will change significantly during the first year of CTM. Inventories will have dropped dramatically, leading to either increased cash or decreased bank loans. This pool of credit or cash will then be available to finance the drive to reach benchmark or become best in the industry. Such goals are attainable only if you engineer out nonessential components and processes or use technology to reduce the time taken by essential activities.

As a side benefit, when inventories cease to be a material factor in a profit-and-loss statement, outsiders can be more confident of the statement's accuracy. Large and material inventories have traditionally served as logical hiding places for poor performances — and sometimes even for good performances. Since inventory valuation is an art, not a science, personal judgment plays an important part in the valuation process. As a result, an inventory value of plus or minus 10 percent is easy to justify. Obviously, 10 percent of $18 million is more material than 10 percent of $3 million.

REDUCTION OF THE WORKING CAPITAL CYCLE

Traditionally, the balance sheet and the source and application of funds have been used to keep track of the working capital requirements. Some companies have also used the cash flow statement. This statement is important in a CTM evolution, because it helps to expand the cycle time concept to include the receipt of payment. To this point, cycle time could be seen as starting with the order and finishing with shipment of the product. However, running in parallel with this process is a working capital cycle that needs to be included in the definition of total business cycle time.

Let's assume that your working capital cycle is 84 days, which includes 42 days from order to shipment and another 42 days to collect the accounts receivable. Suppose you reduce processing cycle time from 42 days to 2 days, while the present customer payment schedule is around 42 days. Then the business cycle time will be 44 days, or the length of time it takes to collect the receivables. How will this scenario affect the working capital flow of funds? Since companies normally pay suppliers in 40 to 45 days, your customers will cover your payments to suppliers.

This arrangement can apply to 50 percent or more of your disbursements. You will need to cover the management and office monthly payroll for about 4 to 6 days and about 6 to 8 days of the shop employees' weekly payroll. While most manufacturers cannot conceive of having such a working capital cycle, we know a company that has had one like it for years. A manufacturer of corrugated boxes gets a customer order ready for delivery in 15 days. It orders raw materials to be delivered during the afternoon of the

14th day, produces the product and delivers it together with an invoice on the 15th day. This company has to contend with key suppliers that also perceive it as a direct competitor. Instead of the usual 30 days credit, the suppliers only allow 15 days. The company's response is to extend only 10 days' credit to its customers, which the customers have paid willingly.

Such working capital targets are unthinkable with a traditional manufacturing process. They are possible in a CTM operation.

INTRODUCTION OF NEW ASSET-VALUATION CRITERIA

In the traditional system, the usual requisition was for a stand-alone piece of equipment, a total process, or a plant. The instinct was to buy excess capacity, the fastest equipment, and (starting in the early 1980s) the most advanced electronic gadgetry available.

Inevitably, the new machines were expensive. Volume of output and costs per widget were the performance measures used to determine payback period. The payback period and amount of capital plus the projected costs of money were plugged into discounted cash flow models, and the project was evaluated and ranked according to priority. In a traditional process, the major emphasis is to determine payback and the money implications of the investment. Since each machine or process is an independent cost center, there is no perceived need to study the impact of the new machine on the whole process.

In a linear flow process, where all the machines are interdependent, the criteria for evaluating new machine purchases are necessarily different. For example, the following questions are critical:

- Is the equipment a replacement? Would the old machine still be useful in a dedicated role?
- What impact will new machines have on the effort to reduce cycle time? Does the machine reduce the time required to do the essential activities and not increase the nonessentials, such as maintenance? Are all the gadgets essential to meet the line requirements? If the machine is

complex, are training courses for operators and maintenance people available? How long and how much investment will be required to get the equipment operating
efficiently?

- Will the machine create or reduce the impact of bottlenecks? Implicit in this question is that if the machine is too
  fast and creates a line-balancing bottleneck, then it is not
  going to help the process. Further, it may be possible to
  get a smaller, less complex machine, that is less expensive
  and does the job better.
- How reliable is the machine? Remember, in a linear flow
  process if one machine breaks down, the whole process
  stops. Reliability is therefore an imperative criterion in the
  evaluation of new equipment. It is better to spend more
  money to get the most reliable machine available.
- Is the machine easy to maintain? If a critical machine's vital
  parts are inaccessible, hampering both lubrication and
  repair, the machine will be a major weakness in a linear
  flow process.

The cost of money is still an important factor in the evaluation process. However, the new criteria are essential because they
insure that the linear flow process is not impeded. Therefore, the
capital budget process must include people who can properly
assess the impact of new equipment on the linear flow process.

SIMPLIFICATION OF INTERNAL CONTROLS

Fast-track cycle time reduction raises a new concern for
finance. As traditional operations became larger and more complex,
control procedures became more essential and more costly. In
CTM operations, however, the complexity diminishes and many of
those procedural controls are exposed as bottlenecks. The main task
is to determine what procedures are essential to assurance that
proper controls are in place. A secondary task is to determine when
to change internal control procedures and reduce the related costs.

Protecting company assets will continue to be a key CFO
responsibility. Only finance can decide which internal controls to

modify and when. To do so, it needs to participate in designing the evolution process so it becomes aware of potential bottlenecks caused by existing internal control procedures and understands the new control tools that are available.

Linear Flow as an Internal Control Tool

Recall the following characteristics of a CTM linear flow process that uses the pull approach:

- Planners will only schedule final assembly. The system will schedule each individual machine from that point on.
- Inventories will be relatively insignificant, and turning over daily. There will be no inventory lying on the shop floor.
- The whole process will be visible from start to finish.
- If the process is not fed properly, it will shut down.
- If the right engineering drawings are not at the right station at the right time, the process will shut down.
- If one station in the process starts producing defects, the process will shut down.

Financial managers will accept the linear flow system as an integral control check only when they can

- appreciate why the system cannot do rework or have pallets of unfinished material on the floor
- determine when the system can replace many of the present inspection points
- determine when inventories are small enough so that the system can replace the old physical controls

Bottlenecks Created by Internal Controls

Some of the most obvious bottlenecks created by traditional controls occur in the following areas:

Secured stores areas. Since these areas are the most glaring bottlenecks, they are usually among the first internal controls to disappear. As part of the linear flow process, bins with small quantities are instead set up close to the operators that need the items. In our experience, pilferage has not been a problem. This is probably because, first, not many units are in the bins at any given time and, second, the units are under the watchful eye of the operators who need them to do their job.

This change is often the first indicator to management that employees are willing and able to take responsibility for company property.

Purchasing and accounts payable. Many purchasing departments have already begun to eliminate some of their internal control bottlenecks. They continue to keep the basic functions of requisitioning, ordering, receiving, and paying for the goods separated, but change the way those functions are performed. For example, they have replaced the purchase order with one blanket order negotiated annually with major suppliers.

As part of that order, both sides agree to an annual quantity of a specified material or component, at a predetermined price and quality, to be delivered daily or weekly as specified on a weekly release. Accounts payable still has to ensure that the company receives the right goods in the right quantity and match this information to supplier invoices. However, instead of filling out a paper form, many companies feed the receiving information into a computer and then match it to the supplier invoice when accounts payable enters it.

Another possible change is to reduce the number of suppliers. As part of the new relationship, the key suppliers will be involved in the product design process, which includes creating the quality standards for their components. Then they will be expected to accept responsibility for meeting those standards. As soon as suppliers demonstrate that they are meeting the quality standards, you can move the receiving location for materials and components from one specific receiving dock to the spot where the material or components enter the process. A line that is operating in proper conjunction with an accredited vendor will provide the assurance that the right quantity is shipped at the right time to the right spot. Quality checks will still be required.

The issue then becomes, Who should do the control checks? In some cases the process itself can provide the necessary internal control checks and balances. For example, suppose all material is delivered daily to the point of use. It is fair to assume that a line with uninterrupted operation is the best indicator that suppliers have met their obligations.

For internal controllers to reach that level of confidence in the system, purchasing, engineering, and quality control must have worked with the supplier to ensure that specifications are right, that tolerances are tighter, and that material and components are meeting those specifications and tolerances.

Capital approval system. Approval of a capital budget item usually requires many signatures. Again, the issue is not *whether an approval process is necessary.* The issue is *how to minimize the approval process and still maintain proper control.* Remember that in a CTM plant the management or approval team, as a group, has to approve beforehand any change requiring an appropriation.

Engineering change process. Engineering change approvals are often roadblocks. In Chapter 4 we saw how Pratt & Whitney dramatically reduced the cycle time necessary to make a simple engineering change by allowing the design engineer to make the decision. The question there was not whether one person should be allowed to make indiscriminate changes to the design. The question was whether all those signatures were essential to the approval process.

The credit approval system. Several companies, including Hewlett-Packard, discovered that their credit-check procedures for new customers constituted a bottleneck. One HP plant was able to reduce its cycle time from 42 days to 2 days. The cycle time was stalled at that level until the credit-check process was reduced to 1 day.

The lesson from each of these areas is to sort out the control procedures in advance, rather than wait until they are bottlenecks. There is time to let the changes evolve naturally, if the controls are considered in parallel with the other cycle time reduction activities.

Moreover, if the thinking is done in parallel, the radical ideas that emerge during the process will seem more sensible.

Toyota provides some idea of just how radical some financial procedures will become in the drive to reduce cycle time. Toyota has a group of suppliers whose quality is so high that Toyota pays them on the basis of the number of finished cars produced during a given period. For example, each car has five tires. Therefore, the tire manufacturer for that model is paid for five tires multiplied by the number of cars shipped during the period. The supplier knows how many tires were shipped. Toyota trusts the quality, and knows that the quantity was correct because the line did not shut down.

The process itself plays a key role, but the functions of ordering, handling, and paying for it are still separate and distinct.

As all the examples indicate, you can eliminate many nonessential activities without jeopardizing internal control. In fact, the new more streamlined controls are likely more trustworthy than the traditional ones, because the system itself becomes an effective control tool.

EMERGENCE OF A NEW COST MODEL

The profit-and-loss statement and the balance sheet are traditional cost models that lose their relevancy in cycle time reduction. Because the impact of cycle time reduction is so dramatic, a more useful model is one that enables managers to see the *expected impact* of changes on profits and working capital requirements. Such a model, which we call an *interactive model*, will also be a valuable control tool.

The DuPont model is an early example of an interactive model. It links the balance sheet and profit-and-loss statements to project the impact on profits or working capital of any change in expense, revenue, asset, or liability. This form of model provides a good overview control of any change. The only problem is that it tends to be prepared in isolation by the finance department rather than being integrated with operations and the budget. We believe that a more useful operating and control model can be developed from the cost system, which people work with day to day.

The Costing System as the Basis of a Financial Model

As you are establishing CTM, you need a trusted cost system that will provide both another control and another incentive to encourage continuous cycle time reduction. However, if one can judge from the derision that most participants in our public seminars heap on their costings, most existing cost systems don't do the job.

Changing Focus of Cost Systems

The focus of the traditional standard cost systems is on direct material and direct labor, with all remaining costs lumped into overheads. In CTM, the focus changes.

Direct materials cost is still allocated to each product.

However, the number of suppliers likely decreases, and blanket orders replace individual purchase orders for all components purchased from major suppliers. Therefore, price changes for materials are easy to spot and adjust.

Direct labor in a CTM plant represents too small a percentage of total cost to be segregated from overhead costs. Furthermore, labor and machine efficiency statistics are irrelevant in a pull linear process, because line balancing is achieved by measures such as having some machines idle occasionally and having operators run one or more machines, or work on cycle time reduction projects or in other areas. Direct labor is not an efficiency measure in CTM.

Overheads become a major item in a CTM plant. However, rather than smearing one lump sum across each product as a percentage of one driver, such as direct labor, you benefit by using more drivers and by adopting activity-based costing practices, which we discuss later in this chapter.

The Changing Role of Cost Systems

The traditional cost system has several roles:

- *It provides a standard against which performance can be measured.* Variances indicate how the plant is performing against those standards.

- *It provides a form of tracking* and therefore control of physical inventories, as the materials and components go through the plant.
- *It appraises inventory for financial statement preparation.* Because inventories have become a significant factor in determining corporate profits, inventory valuation has also become more important.
- *It serves as an aid in pricing the product.* However, since most companies distrust traditional cost models, they seldom use them to establish prices.

In CTM, the four roles of traditional costing change (see Table 7-1):

- *Variances* become irrelevant. Standards are not used to judge performance.
- *Tracking* becomes redundant. Reduced cycle time means reduced inventories. As well, control in a pull system remains tight, because if the right material is not at the right place at the right time, the process stops.
- *Inventory valuations* diminish in importance, because inventories become relatively insignificant as dollar figures on the balance sheet. The product cost figures are used to value finished goods, and a rough pipeline valuation is used for the kanban or work-in-process figures. Raw material is valued at invoice cost.

	Traditional	CTM
Variances	Vital measure	Irrelevant
Tracking	Only WIP control	No value — no WIP
Inventory Valuations	Important, since inventory large	Less important, since inventory small
Pricing	Guide only	Useful guide and control

Table 7-1. Costing Roles in Traditional and CTM Operations

- *Costing as an aid to pricing* encourages employees to think of cost accounting as dynamic and proactive rather than isolated and reactive. This new role is an outgrowth of the target costing process used by cost-estimating engineers in new product development.

Target Costing

The first step in deciding whether to build new product X is to determine whether it will make a profit. Two targets are set at the outset. The first is the selling price that marketing believes will be appropriate, and the second is the profit expected from the sale of each unit of this product. Suppose the selling price for the product is $1.00 and the expected profit is 20 cents. That leaves 80 cents to build and ship each unit of new product (see Table 7-2).

Once a firm cost target has been established, the design and cost-estimating engineers develop a cost profile of the new product. Design creates a parts list. The cost estimates are developed from a series of "looks like" discussions between design and cost engineers. ("This component looks like component X, is that right?" "No, it's closer to that new variation of X that we are using in product A.") Suppose the cost estimates are within the 80-cent limit and the company decides to build the product. Few North American companies compare the detailed target costs to the actual costs of making the product. However, some companies, such as Honda and Canon, assume that from the time a product is conceived to the time it has to be redesigned or pulled off the market there will be a continuous effort to reduce the costs of manufacturing. Starting with the first quarter that prod-

Target sales price	$1.00
Target profit / unit	.20
Maximum cost / unit	.80

Table 7-2. Sample Cost Target

uct X is manufactured, they have quarterly meetings to encourage this process. One Honda general manager even uses this meeting to keep control of engineering changes. While he wants to be assured that the changes will not affect safety and quality standards, he also expects that the changes will reduce costs. The quarterly meeting is where that expectation is discussed.

Target costing does have one weakness. Integral to it is the assumption that the existing cost model reflects an accurate allocation of overheads. Our experience suggests that where there is more than one product or family of products, this is not often the case. Another approach — activity-based costing — allocates overheads better.

Activity-Based Costing

Activity-based costing (ABC) is the most promising alternative cost model for a company that is converting to CTM.[1] It is compatible with the objectives of managing by cycle time partly because it can provide a more accurate cost allocation of overheads. Just as important, it can be developed into a model that fulfills the new roles of encouraging and complementing the cycle time reduction process and assisting in new product introduction.

The Benefit of ABC: A Case Study. The impact that ABC can have on the strategic thinking of a company is exemplified by the experience of the John Deere Component and Works (JDCW).[2] The machining department of JDCW produces machine parts. In an average year it produces about 1,500 different parts. JDCW was a captive supplier to its parent, John Deere, until the collapse of commodity prices in the 1980s led to the most sustained agricultural crisis since the Great Depression. To promote increased efficiency, John Deere allowed its divisions both to sell their output to outside firms and to purchase inputs from external suppliers. As the head of engineering noted: "We always made all the components for tractors, so we ran lots of part numbers but never really looked at costs of individual parts. What was important was the efficiency of the whole rather than the efficiency of making parts."

The shift from captive supplier to open competition altered management's primary focus from overall efficiency to competition at the individual product level.

Motivated by the shift in strategy, JDCW submitted bids on 275 of the 635 parts John Deere offered for bid in late 1984. The 275 parts were those for which JDCW had manufacturing capability and that were needed in volumes large enough to benefit from the efficiencies of its multispindle machines. JDCW won only 20 percent of the bids, however, with many of the lost bids going to other Deere divisions. JDCW managers found the low success rate disturbing since they had bid aggressively for this business.

Using ABC principles, the managers did a detailed study of the production process flow. They learned that the use of overhead resources was associated with six types of support activities: direct labor support, machine operation, machine setup, material handling, production order processing, and parts administration. They assigned the costs of these activities to the products, using direct labor dollars, machine hours, setup hours, loads of material moved, production orders, and part numbers, respectively. The overhead that could not be associated with products was segregated and prorated to products based on their nonmaterial cost to date.

The new activity-based cost system reported product costs that differed from those reported by the unit-based system it replaced. As expected, it showed that those products consuming relatively small amounts of labor, machine hours, and materials dollars, or those produced in small batches, were less profitable than they thought. For example, the overhead assigned to some products doubled, whereas the overhead assigned to others decreased by 20 percent. The shifts in reported costs matched the expectations of management, though the magnitude of the shifts was greater than expected. As the division manager commented, "Parts we suspected were undercosted turned out to be even more expensive than we thought." As a result, JDCW managers widely adopted ABC practices for decision making. They used product costs reported by the activity-based system to prepare both internal and external customer bids. As the manufacturing superintendent commented, "We are more confident now about our quote prices. And because activity-based costing more properly penalizes low-volume products, we now know which business we don't want." Although this case makes the point that ABC allocates the overheads more effectively than unit-based systems, it also seems to support the traditional concept that short runs are inefficient. However, JDCW had neither reduced changeover times to insignificance nor adopted the other CTM practices. If it had done so, it would probably have been able to efficiently produce even the low-quantity products.

Implementing ABC. In ABC, the strategy is to trace the activities back to the product that requires those activities and then assign the costs that are related to the activities. This can be done on a macro or micro basis depending on the importance of the expense.

First, focus on the large and significant costs. Next, look at the activities that created those costs. Consider these questions:

- Should the activities be traced to specific products? If they relate to only a few products, then the costs should be specifically allocated. Warranty costs are a good example. Logic would suggest that if you have a mix of new products, built-to-order products, and standard products, then the new products and built-to-order products should cause more warranty activity than standard products. Therefore, an activity analysis to determine which products are creating the warranty expense will provide a more reliable guide for allocating the warranty cost. However, if the warranty cost is not significant, it may not matter how you allocate it.
- Is there a specific driver that reflects how the cost should be allocated? For example, the sales expense might be allocated on the basis of sales dollars, number of units sold, or number of orders processed. If one product is a cash cow requiring little marketing to bring in substantial orders, then its burden of the sales cost should be less than that allocated to a new product for which a lot of sales effort is required to establish the distribution network. Indeed, the share of total sales cost should be inversely proportional to the number of orders or sales dollars generated, or whatever other measure is appropriate.

- Will a traditional driver such as direct labor, processing time, machine hours, or materials provide an equitable way of allocating a pool of cost? The answer is yes: if a traditional driver is appropriate, use it. The problem with standard costing is not that it uses direct labor as a driver, but that direct labor tends to be the only driver it uses.
- In a company that is just initiating a cycle time reduction process, ABC principles can be incorporated into a simulation model that provides several benefits:

  1. It can allocate costs to products on a more equitable basis. As a result of the increased international competitive pressure in the 1980s, many make/buy decisions were made. Some companies have reassessed those decisions using ABC and determined that they were poor ones.
  2. It can provide a baseline or existing cost by product so you can track the impact of cycle time reduction on that cost. Most people want to know in dollars what the improvement possibilities are. With ABC it is quite easy to calculate the cost.
  3. It can be used to introduce a proactive use of costings that encourages continuous cost cutting.
  4. It can be used to develop pools of costs associated with nonessential activities so that you can show the cost reductions expected from eliminating those activities and reducing cycle time. The ability to anticipate cost reductions provides an incentive to the group to press on with cycle time reduction.

     As well, the ability to model expectations makes it easier for management to allocate resources to cycle time reduction projects.
  5. Used in conjunction with PERT or critical path charts, an ABC model can help managers and employees handle instability, by helping them to anticipate certain events and the impact of those events on profits.

As a result of their participation in cycle time reduction, CFOs will discover that there is a broader proactive role for them in a company managed by cycle time. Also, by understanding and supporting the conversion to CTM, they can ensure that internal control procedures will neither be compromised nor impede the cycle time reduction process. Finally, if they use a simulation model that incorporates ABC concepts they can anticipate destabilizing events, and therefore help the company and their colleagues to evolve in a controlled and orderly way.

NOTES

1. The discussion of ABC owes much to Robin Cooper's and Robert Kaplan's "Measure Costs Right: Make the Right Decisions," *Harvard Business Review*, September-October 1988, p. 96.
2. Harvard Business School, Cases 9-187-107 and 9-187-108, John Deere Component Works A and B.

8

The Implementation Process

Many companies are beginning to understand the rationale behind Cycle Time Management. However, few have actually implemented CTM, and even fewer have done so on a fast track.

The reader will leave this chapter with a strong impression of a tightly controlled participative approach, one that involves *all* employees in a major change in the way they do business. If management is prepared to focus the resources, it can greatly accelerate the normal process of change.

Used correctly, the implementation guidelines outlined here have proved to be very effective when applied across an organization. They should assist you in getting your company on the fast-track approach.

The CTM implementation process has two objectives:

- To involve all employees in continuous cycle time reduction and continuous business improvement
- To provide an orderly and controlled change process for the whole organization

The CTM implementation process generates an integrated businesswide CTM evolution plan with cycle time improvement as its main focus. The process facilitates in-depth initial planning as well as ongoing planning and tracking throughout the evolution plan's execution. It outlines how to evaluate the organization by conducting an implementation risk assessment against a series of prerequisites and then forming teams to generate the actual CTM evolution plan. The implementation process then provides a mechanism for activating and controlling the various programs and projects that are identified in the evolution plan.

Let us assume that the decisionmakers in your business already understand the CTM concept and can envision its benefits. What we provide here is a proven, detailed process for implementing CTM and doing so on a fast-track. Keep in mind that this is only a process and, although you should use external support to "stay on the track," it is the organization itself that must drive in this race.

TRADITIONAL CHANGE
VERSUS CTM EVOLUTION

The CTM road map and implementation process feature early involvement at all levels, a formal project structure, a management approval and problem escalation process, and a method of developing strong participation at all levels both for developing the plan and then executing it.

This is in contrast with a traditional change approach, in which managers do most of the planning and the work force must adjust to change instead of being fully involved in planning, implementing, and managing it.

THE CTM IMPLEMENTATION
ROAD MAP: A GENERAL REVIEW

The CTM implementation road map outlines the total CTM fast-track implementation process from the moment of executive awareness to the final outcome of continuous improvement (see Figure 8-1).

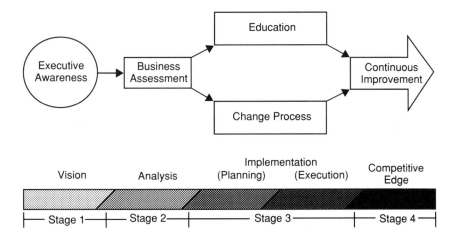

Figure 8-1. The Road Map to CTM Implementation

It defines four stages:

1. *Vision:* This starts to develop through CTM education that fosters executive awareness of the CTM concept and the opportunities that it represents.
2. *Analysis:* A formal business assessment ensures that all the necessary prerequisites and requirements for a successful conversion to CTM are identified ahead of time and that most if not all have been provided.
3. *Implementation:* This stage encompasses a tightly controlled sequence of 12 steps divided into planning and execution phases. It outlines how education, planning, and execution can be integrated into full-scale development of the evolution plan.

   Since CTM is such a radical departure from traditional operating practices, a total commitment to a sustained effort toward change is a prime prerequisite for successful implementation.
4. *Competitive Edge:* At the completion of the CTM implementation process, CTM will have become "a way of life."

As a result, the organization will be able to continue the cycle time reduction process on its own and ensure that the company maintains its competitive edge via continuous improvement.

STAGE 1: VISION/EXECUTIVE AWARENESS

Once the executives understand the CTM concept, they can envisage how to apply it to their own organization (see Figure 8-2). Common to all programs for CTM are

- the use of cycle time as the measure of productivity
- a goal of total business linear flow
- a focus on people as the drivers of the improvement process

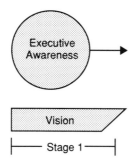

Figure 8-2. Stage 1 of CTM Implementation

This vision embraces not only the direct operation but also all support functions, the management structure, and the operational organization. As noted earlier, CTM is not just a series of engineering projects to reorganize the manufacturing and distribution processes, or yet another look at the office organization and paper flow, or an assessment of the company's procedures and practices. It is all of these — and more. That is why traditional project or task forces or special corporate program activities are insufficient for the implementation of CTM. What is demanded is a radically new way of thinking about the company's operating practices and business cycle.

Imagine a traditional business with a long cycle time and large inventories of finished goods and work-in-process. The operating approach in such a situation is to forecast stock levels, build to those levels, and ship from that stock. By comparison, a CTM operation designs and manufactures the same products in a short cycle time with a far more streamlined linear flow, starting with a much more responsive real-time order-entry system. Cycle time within the process is short enough that customer requests can be built to order from the raw material stage. Thus, customer delivery requirements are fully satisfied while finished goods and WIP inventories remain limited. If the suppliers are included in this new approach, the quantity of raw materials onhand can be reduced substantially as well.

The CTM Issues

During the period of executive awareness building, several points become clear:

1. CTM represents a radical change in business operating practices. Such a change can be a threatening and humbling experience for everyone, especially the management team.
2. CTM is not a technology. Thus it represents a departure from traditional, technology-based solutions to business and operating process problems.
3. CTM cannot be programmed or contracted into place. Companies converting to CTM cannot "bring in an expert" who opens a kit bag and applies a packaged or semicustomized solution to their problems.
4. CTM requires an *implementation process*. CTM involves *all* people in the organization. This entails careful planning at all levels.
5. Before engaging in fast-track implementation of CTM, you must ensure that everyone in the organization understands CTM. This requires education and training. Supporting the education program should be a management team that:

- understands CTM concepts
- has a vision of and commitment to the total business linear flow process
- knows what facilitation skills are required for the 12-step implementation process

STAGE 2: ANALYSIS/BUSINESS ASSESSMENT

Once a clear vision of CTM exists within the management team, the next step is to undertake a CTM business assessment (see Figure 8-3). This will determine what specific requirements are needed to prepare the company for implementation of fast-track cycle time. It is important to determine the organization's present level of cycle time performance and measure its readiness to proceed against the CTM implementation prerequisites. On the basis of this business assessment you establish the costs of CTM implementation.

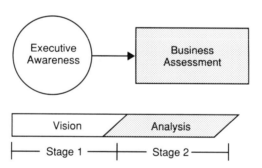

Figure 8-3. Stage 2 of CTM Implementation

The CTM business assessment readies the organization for launching the CTM process. No one wants a bad launch. If you are going to involve everyone in the launch process, it had better work: close attention to avoiding the risks of a bad launch is vital to your credibility as a member of the management team.

The first step in making a business assessment is to take a penetrating look at the present organization. The CTM approach is to interview representatives of all functions to determine what their concerns are. The second step is to determine how existing improvement projects involving automation, computer-integrated manufacturing, quality, statistical process control training, and CTM education can be integrated into one implementation process. The information gathered during the first two steps provides a data base for determining not only the costs of implementation, but also the risks.

Planning for Implementation

Most traditional managers are oriented to action, not planning. In CTM, however, the emphasis is on planning (see Figure 8-4). Therefore, managers must resist the temptation to rush into an ineffective implementation, no matter how much frustration this creates initially. Managers must also avoid any appearance of frustration during these preparation activities. Everyone on the team must display confidence in the ability of the organization to plan and implement the CTM vision.

The objectives of the 12-step CTM planning and implementation process in Stage 3 are:

- to involve everybody in the evolution process as quickly as possible
- to ensure that the organization takes a disciplined approach to planning the evolution
- to implement the evolution in an orderly fashion

This is a major undertaking. Take the time to review the prerequisites for CTM, Stage 3 during the analysis (Stage 2).

An important task during the planning stage will be to measure the risks that may be involved in implementing CTM. To do this you need to be aware of the prerequisites of Stage 3.

The CTM prerequisites of Stage 3.

1. The first requirement is a *committed and enlightened management team* willing to do in-depth planning and forestalling any rush for change.

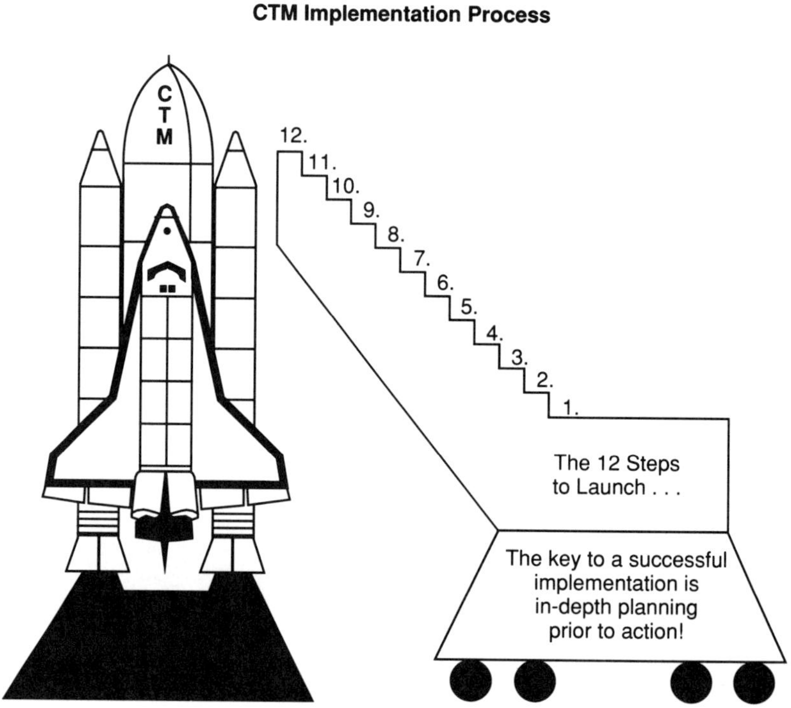

CTM Implementation Process

The 12 Steps to Launch . . .

The key to a successful implementation is in-depth planning prior to action!

Figure 8-4. Planning Is the Key to Successful Implementation of CTM

Unfortunately, this is the area where most organizations fail. It is our experience that most management teams are not perceived by the rest of the organization as enlightened and committed or even as cohesive. This presents a distinct problem: many of the discrete operating practices that have prevented cohesion in the past need at this point to be reconsidered. A common understanding of where the risks for implementation reside is thus essential.

It is important, too, that every member of the management team have an opportunity to generate discussion on any issue that he or she believes affects the team's commitment and enlightenment. This calls for specific facilitation skills not usually available inside organizations.

2. *The management team must have the authority, ability, and commitment to communicate the CTM principles* throughout the entire organization: that is, to educate.
3. There must be *sufficient allocation of resources* to support the education, training, and project activity. Sound CTM education is required at all levels prior to CTM evolution planning and execution.
4. *A strong participative culture* at all levels is essential. This must be *demonstrated* by management.
5. *Leaders must have project management and facilitation skills* to organize the projects defined and ensure that the involvement is correctly facilitated via the planning activity.
6. Leaders must be able to manage all changes in the processes and operating practices of the organization. Thus the following conditions must exist:
   • Communication across the whole organization
   • Total involvement in the changes at all levels
   • Reinforcement of the need for change
   • Clear and early visibility of the changes
   • A demonstrated fear-free environment (thus, perception that the changes are necessary and well managed)
   • Trust among all levels in the organization
7. *Education at all levels* is necessary before any change is undertaken or people become involved in planning the changes. This must focus upon the CTM concept, the implementation tools, and the project management and facilitation skills.

The Risk Decision. Although the CTM implementation process can proceed if some of the prerequisites are not yet in place, any attempt to implement CTM will fail if there is not complete and absolute management commitment to maintain the momentum of the evolution.

At the completion of the business assessment, the organization must determine whether more groundwork needs to be done or whether it is in position to launch the fast-track implementation process.

CTM implementation — How much will it cost us? The real question is, how much will it cost us if we *don't* implement CTM? It is important to keep in mind that most of the CTM implementation costs can be self-funded — that is, the internal costs can be absorbed by the spare work hours that can be found within any organization. In addition, most organizations get productivity improvement immediately from externally supported CTM education and facilitation.

Furthermore, because of the CTM concept of simplification, little actual capital expenditure is necessary in the early phases of the implementation process; most organizations are able to bury these low costs in their existing expense budgets.

Are we ready? Let's assume your organization meets sufficient prerequisites and can absorb the initial costs. It is now ready to embark on Stage 3 of the fast track to CTM.

STAGE 3: IMPLEMENTATION

As the 12-step implementation process unfolds, the need for operational and procedural change must be induced into the minds of all the people in the organization. Through conceptual education and training, a paradigm shift is achieved, and fuels the evolution planning activities.

The 12-Step Implementation Process

The CTM implementation process, or evolution plan, consists of 12 steps divided into planning and execution phases. Three control and maintenance steps occur throughout the execution phase (see Table 8-1).

Steps 1 through 7 are planning steps and consume the most energy in terms of building the organization's CTM team structure and defining the evolution plan for CTM implementation. Steps 8 and 9 are execution steps and initiate change through ongoing tactical planning. Steps 10, 11, and 12 are maintenance and control steps to ensure that CTM is continuously monitored and maintained.

Table 8-1. The 12-Step Implementation Process

Step Activity	Output	Purpose	Responsibility
Plan			
1. Approval team kickoff	Mission statement	Define goals	Management team
2. Planning forum kickoff	Position analysis	Define as-is situation	Senior staff members
3. Review team kickoff	Forum teams	Focus planning effort	Senior staff members
4. Review team planning	Detailed plans	Define actions	Senior staff members
5. Formalize evolution plan	Define evolution projects	Single coordinated plan	Forum members
6. Management approval	Approve plan	Buy-in at all levels	Approval and forum teams
7. Communicate evolution plan	Communicate plan	Ensure plan is understood	Approval and forum teams
Execute			
8. Program kickoff	Start to implement	Schedule and coordinate	Program and project leaders
9. Project kickoff	First team meeting	Implement project plan	Project leader and team members
Control and Maintenance			
10. Management approval meeting	Approval project phase	Ensure correct management control	Program and project leaders approval team
11. Monthly evolution plan/ program review	Review evolution plan status	Ensure correct priorities and resources	Program and project leaders approval team
12. Quarterly communication sessions	Ensure plan's progress is understood by everyone	Continued commitment to evolution activities	Management approval team

The CTM implementation process integrates all of the organization's present and future projects and activities associated with operational improvement and change into one continuous cycle time improvement plan (hence the term *evolution plan*). Obviously, it is easier to manage one integrated improvement process than many sometimes unrelated projects. Further, since there is now only one main performance benchmark — cycle time — management's ability to prioritize projects and allocate resources will be vastly improved and simplified.

This change implementation process is self-sustaining, provides a stable and reinforcing platform for change, and builds trust across the organization. It can be applied either to a vertical slice of the organization or globally across the company. It provides a meaningful active role for all involved in the changes, from the president to the direct operators. This process provides self-sufficiency and is relatively independent of the existing management system.

The CTM Implementation Time Frame

Some organizations have been able to move through the first seven planning steps in about 12 to 14 weeks. An additional 8 to 12 weeks is required to complete the execution and control/maintenance steps adequately. Therefore, to fully install and make the CTM process "a way of life" takes between 20 and 26 weeks. Most organizations start to see the benefits within the first year (see Figure 8-5).

Tangible benefits for most organizations will become evident within the first 6 to 12 months after starting the CTM implementation process.

Intangible benefits such as improved communication and an increase in employee involvement start after Step 2 or 3.

The CTM Implementation Structure and Organization

Several new functions need to be established as part of the CTM implementation process (see Figure 8-6). The evolution

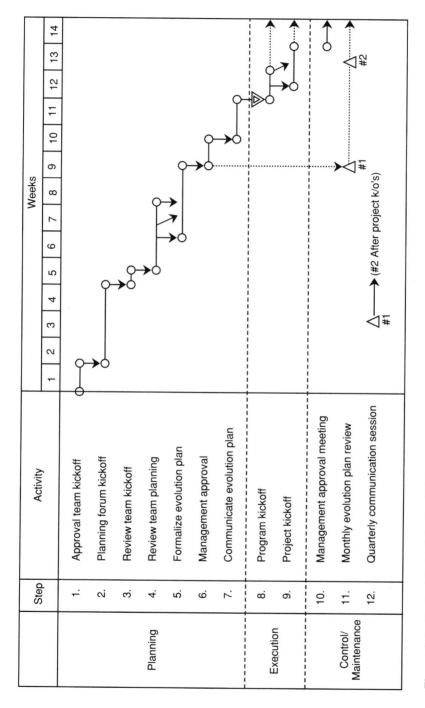

Figure 8-5. Typical Schedule for CTM Implementation

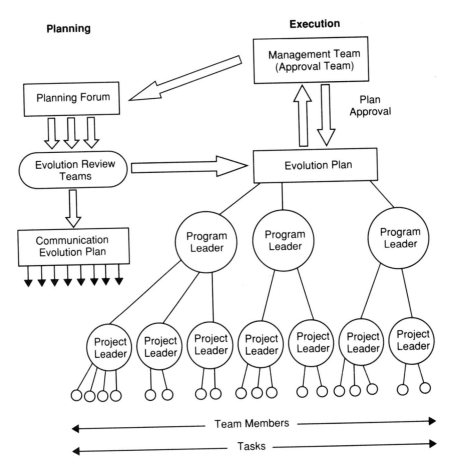

Figure 8-6. Evolution Plan Team Structure

plan team structure will be explained as we outline each of the 12 steps.

STAGE 3A: PLANNING PHASE

The implementation of CTM begins with a period of detailed planning, the first seven steps of the 12-step process (see Figure 8-7).

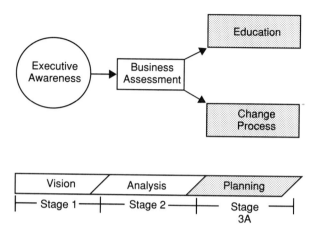

Figure 8-7. Stage 3A of CTM Implementation (Planning Phase)

Step 1: The Management Approval Team Kickoff

The approval team kickoff meeting initiates the CTM implementation *planning* process (see Figure 8-8).

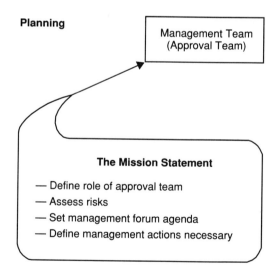

Figure 8-8. Step 1: Approval Team Kickoff Meeting

The role of the approval team. It is important for members of the approval team to understand their new role in the CTM evolution planning activity. Instead of directing employees to plan and execute change, they now approve plans developed by evolution team members from all departments (see Figure 8-9). This shift in management roles must be accompanied by the general perception that a new management style and process for change has been put in place. The importance of this perception cannot be overstressed.

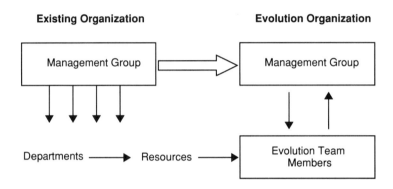

Figure 8-9. Management Role in Traditional versus CTM Organization

Thus, in Step 1 the management team must evolve from a direction-giving authority into an approval team to manage the change. The replacement of *direction* with *approval* is an important element in empowering people to plan and execute change.

Moreover, the new approach to improving business operating processes involves the use of cross-functional resources, which would not be possible under the old system of direct control demarcated by departments.

Risk assessment. Another major item for discussion at Step 1 is the review of the implementation risks. Although a discussion of risks starts during the review of the business assessment, it is important for the approval team to evaluate the CTM implementation risks collectively one last time. To ensure that all concerns about risks can be exposed and discussed fruitfully, have an outsider facilitate this meeting. The facilitator can guide the communication and help develop a cohesive management team that is ready and able to operate in its new role as the approval team in the CTM environment.

Remember that once you decide to proceed to Step 2 it is more difficult to stop the process without loss of credibility (hence the need for the risk assessment).

Preparation for Step 2. The approval team carries out several tasks that prepare the way for Step 2. It creates a draft mission statement, which provides a strategic direction only. In addition, the approval team decides how this draft mission statement is to be communicated to the planning forum.

Keep in mind that although agreement may be achieved at this level, the mission statement is still considered a draft so that the other levels of the organization can modify it.

- It selects the members of the planning forum, who will undertake the bulk of the evolution planning.
- It approves the CTM coordinator and establishes the job description for this role.
- It helps the CTM coordinator develop the agenda for Step 2 — the planning forum kickoff meeting. If any management actions are necessary prior to Step 2 these are noted and actions and responsibilities are developed. Such an action might be the establishment of some initial organizations or the allocation of resources that would enable Step 2 to start.

New roles and responsibilities. The *management approval team* is composed of members of the present management team. But the approval team's function (and therefore its meetings) must be kept separate from the management team's existing day-to-day activities. The approval team's role is to establish the implementation process, allocate resources to it, and approve each step and change throughout the process.

The *CTM coordinator* is a new position created by the approval team. It requires good people skills and credibility with employees at all levels. The role is one of influence rather than power. The coordinator should be on the approval team. He or she will chair the management forum and guide and support the review teams during development of the evolution plan and the project teams during the CTM implementation.

The coordinator needs to be full-time for the first seven steps and part-time thereafter for the first year of the implementation.

The *planning forum* is composed of second-line managers and key employees. Its scope, mandate, and membership are established by the approval team. Its role is to create the evolution plan. Its process is to delegate the job of defining specific cycle time reduction opportunities to the review teams.

Step 2: The Planning Forum Kickoff

The planning forum is basically a cross-functional team that, after receiving the necessary CTM training, undertakes to develop

- a positional analysis of the existing macro opportunities for reducing cycle time
- an evolution plan that focuses on those opportunities

The forum also establishes smaller review teams and delegates to them the responsibility for defining the micro opportunities within their particular areas of focus. It then develops the evolution plan (see Figure 8-10).

At the first meeting of the planning forum, members perform several tasks:

- They update the draft mission statement from the approval team.
- They estimate the overall business cycle time, starting from the placement of an order for a product (or service) and ending with the receipt of payment for that product (or service).

The forum may have the mandate to consider some or all of the five cycle time loops:

1. Make/ship
2. New product introduction
3. Supply management
4. Distribution
5. Strategic business development

For each cycle time loop:

- They calculate the baseline, entitlement, and benchmark cycle times (defined in Chapter 5). Even though the calculations are approximate at this point, they provide reference points and targets for the next level of planning teams.
- They segment the detailed macro charts, with their baseline, entitlement, and benchmark estimates into "areas of focus."
- They create review teams for each area of focus with a definition of the scope and mandate to document the cycle time reduction opportunities in the area of focus.
- They select review team members. Most people enjoy this task, which is an important part of the team-building process. It is also the first step to building personal commitment to the evolution plan. Generally, members for these

Planning

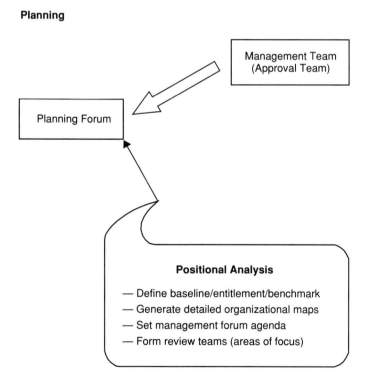

Management Team
(Approval Team)

Planning Forum

Positional Analysis

— Define baseline/entitlement/benchmark
— Generate detailed organizational maps
— Set management forum agenda
— Form review teams (areas of focus)

Figure 8-10. Step 2: Planning Forum Kickoff

review teams should be chosen from the forum membership; however, other members of the organization may be nominated as well if they are judged likely to make a strong contribution. These new members must be educated in the CTM approach before joining the review teams. The teams then select a team leader who must have been part of the forum before joining the review team.

- They establish a series of dates for the review team kickoff meetings.

The CTM coordinator's role. While these are forum activities, it is the CTM coordinator that must provide the support and coordination. Leading these activities requires strong facilitation skills, including a clear vision of the CTM goals and planning principles and a sound knowledge of the implementation agenda.

An *external facilitator* will probably be necessary to assist the coordinator in developing the evolution plan and leading the planning activity.

Step 3: Review Team Kickoff

After every review team member has received the necessary CTM education, each team is launched on its activity. Each ensures that its responsibility is clear and acceptable to all (see Figure 8-11).

Next, the team reviews the key planning principles and objectives:

- The ultimate goal is to survive and make money by satisfying customers (internal as well as external).
- The internal objective is to create a linear business flow by eliminating non-value-added activities and simplifying existing process and product designs.
- Improvement must be continuous.
- People drive the evolution process.

Then the teams review their specific areas of focus, define the information to be gathered by studying the existing information gathered, and develop an action list.

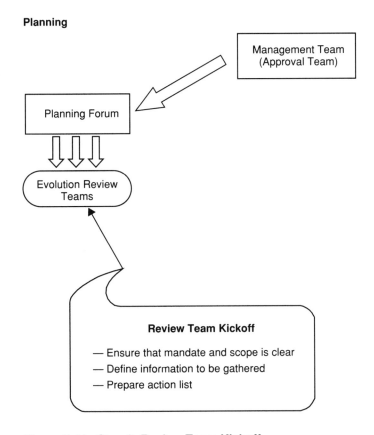

Planning

Figure 8-11. Step 3: Review Team Kickoff

Step 4: Review Team Planning

The number and duration of review teams' meetings will depend on how much analysis and review effort is necessary to expose the impediments to cycle time reduction and define ways of eliminating them. *The review teams should not develop detailed plans for solving these problems but rather should describe projects that define the problems, giving clear scopes and mandates to eliminate the impediments* (see Figure 8-12).

Obviously, both the review team leader and the CTM coordinator must have (at a minimum) some project leadership and problem-solving skills. At this stage an external facilitator with these skills can be used. Eventually, however, everyone who leads a project team in the execution phase of the evolution plan will need these skills.

As part of the CTM education, members of the review team will be trained in the use of the CTM implementation tools. The two new basic tools required for the planning phase are organizational mapping and cycle time measurement.

Organizational mapping involves flowcharting the cycle time process starting at the macro level and then segmenting the map down to a deeper level of detail. (See Chapter 9 for a detailed description of this mapping process and two examples of maps.)

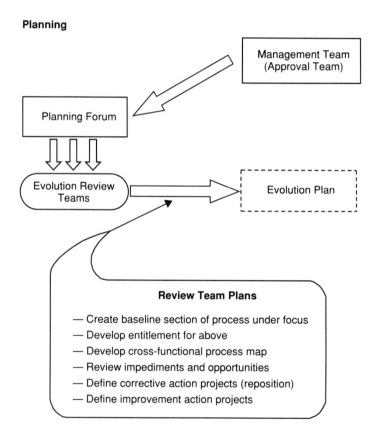

Figure 8-12. Step 4: Review Team Planning

Once the detailed maps for each review team's area of focus are developed, the teams use *cycle time measurement* to quantify these elemental cycle times and identify the cycle time improvements possible and the impediments to making these improvements. (See Chapter 5 for details on the second CTM tool.)

After defining the impediments, the review teams devise CTM projects to eliminate or minimize these impediments. In general, two kinds of projects emerge:

- Corrective action projects that correct basic problems in the existing process (such as lack of procedures or working standards)
- Improvement action projects that activate change or simplify the existing process (such as a departmental reorganization or a new office plan or plant layout)

An *area of focus* might be a paint finish rework loop, which through mapping was found to be a large cycle time impediment to releasing the product to the shipping dock.

A *corrective action project* might be an effort to develop improved workmanship standards, improve the feedback loop to the operators causing the rework, and catch the quality problem when the paint is being applied.

An *improvement action project* in the same scenario might be an effort to prevent the defect from occurring by changing or improving the paint process.

Some of the impediments *will not* be so obvious. In such cases the review teams need to use problem-solving tools to define the impediments and scope out the nature of the projects that will eliminate them.

Review teams can quantify each project's contribution to change in the specific business process by measuring its impact on cycle time, using the second CTM tool. Teams can then determine the contribution to improving cycle time or quality or the costs of doing business across the review teams' areas of focus. Teams insert this projected improvement into the evolution plan by identifying an evolution project for implementation.

In most cycle time improvement programs, companies can achieve almost 80 percent of the cycle time reductions by reaching entitlement (the cycle time achievable without a large investment of capital) and therefore will require minimum capital investment. Moreover, simple rather than complex capital intensive projects become the order of the day.

Step 5: Formalize Evolution Plan

After each review team has developed its list of projects and completed the analysis, the management forum is reconvened to review each team's findings and list the projects that they have identified for input into the evolution plan (see Figure 8-13).

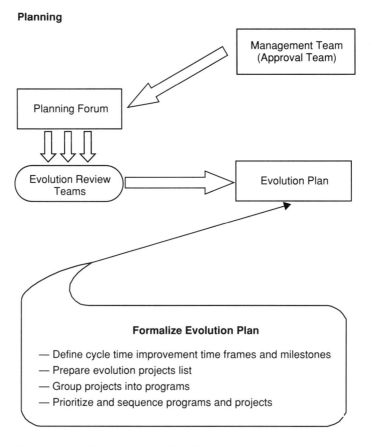

Planning

Management Team (Approval Team)

Planning Forum

Evolution Review Teams

Evolution Plan

Formalize Evolution Plan

— Define cycle time improvement time frames and milestones
— Prepare evolution projects list
— Group projects into programs
— Prioritize and sequence programs and projects

Figure 8-13. Step 5: Formalize Evolution Plan

Review team project rationalization. Some commonality of problems (and therefore projects) will probably exist across review teams. Thus, the planning forum should work toward rationalizing the total list of projects for maximum implementation efficiency. The categorizing of impediments and the cross-functional mapping provides the justification for project rationalization. In addition, the CTM coordinator must ensure that each review team's point of view and project priorities are portrayed fairly. Project rationalization is a sometimes complex task that requires *strong facilitation skills.*

Cycle time reduction time frames. Another forum task is to determine how long each of the projects will take to complete and on that basis to develop a cycle time reduction curve marked with a series of milestones (see Figure 8-14). When developing this curve, the forum might take into account the sequence or priority of each project.

Project groupings. To ensure that each project team has the correct level of support while it moves through the various phases, the forum must group similar projects under a single program. For example, all projects with a quality improvement mandate might be grouped under a program on quality improvement. Similarly, all projects undertaking shop-floor or office relayout might be grouped under one program.

Leading the program must be a member of the approval team. This will ensure that at least one member of the approval team is aware of the specific project activities and allows some focus on near-term resource constraint and other considerations specific to the project.

The role of the program leader should not be confused with that of the project leader. The program leader is involved in the kickoff of projects grouped under that program, but will play a remote role unless the project leader requests otherwise. (More detail on the roles of program and project leaders is provided in the sections on Steps 8 and 9.) For purposes of this step, the forum members nominate from their approval team ranks the various

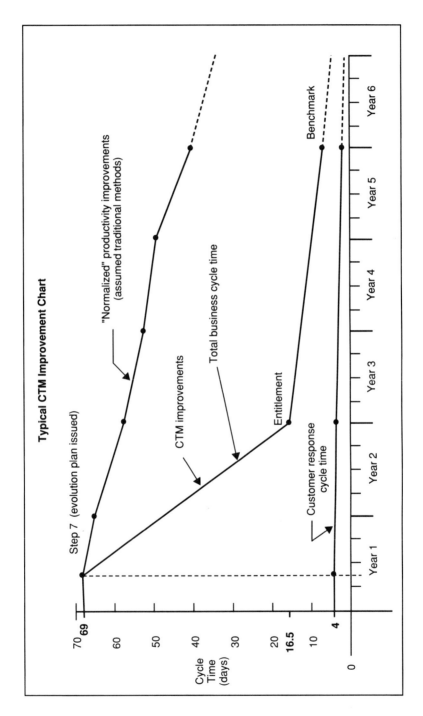

Figure 8-14. Example of a Cycle Time Reduction Curve

program leaders. These nominations are formalized in the evolution plan. This novel approach, which might be called inverse delegation, helps to build a sense of ownership for the evolution plan at all levels.

The program/project structure is a hierarchy of tasks dedicated to the planning, execution, and control of continuous improvement. It is separate and distinct from the normal departmental organization structure (see Figure 8-15). This arrangement creates an effective matrix management system that serves the day-to-day operating needs and also the management of change.

Identification of program and project leaders. Before getting the plan approved, the forum lists the names of the leaders for each program and project. Usually, enthusiasm for the evolution plan naturally results in identification of key project team members as well.

The evolution plan content. At the completion of this stage, the CTM coordinator — with support from the whole forum — will have generated a formal CTM evolution plan with the following characteristics:

1. It contains a proposed final mission statement.
2. It includes strategies for CTM implementation in the form of a listing of programs and projects that have been structured and ranked according to priority. Where possible, the formal plan should contain all the rationales (mapping and implementation information) that support the selection of the projects.
3. It ranks all projects according to importance. It is not unusual for 100 projects or more to be defined. The CTM coordinator should focus particularly on the sequence of the top 20 or 30 projects. This is not to say that only these projects will see completion, but to suggest that some projects must receive priority. In the course of CTM evolution *all* projects will be completed.

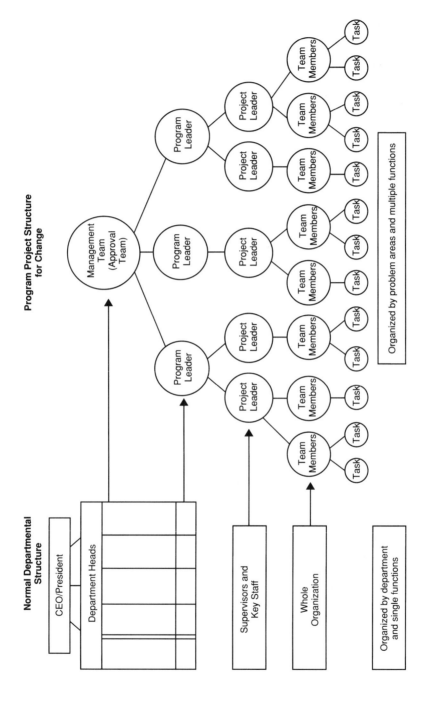

Figure 8-15. CTM Management System

Step 6: Management Approval of Evolution Plan

When the forum has documented and agreed on the evolution plan, the approval team meets to approve it (see Figure 8-16). This is a major event in the CTM implementation process and may take more than one day to complete.

The evolution plan should contain project plans that nominate at least the project leaders and proposed program leaders. In addition, it should define the scope and mandate of the implementation effort, noting cycle time improvement milestones and time frames. If possible, it should identify the central or core members of each project team.

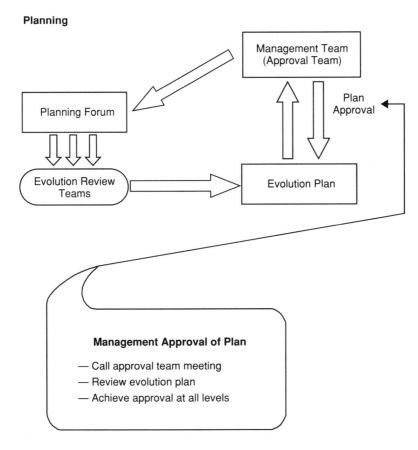

Figure 8-16. Step 6: Management Approval of Evolution Plan

Who should attend? Ideally, everyone who has participated in generating the evolution plan should be present at approval team meetings. (There could be as many as 100 people, depending on the size of the organization.) At a minimum, all members of the approval team and the planning forum must attend.

Agenda. The agenda for the approval team meeting will vary, but in general the first item is a review of the proposed mission statement, followed by presentations from each review team. Next, the CTM coordinator presents the program/project structure, after which the forum lists proposed projects in order of priority.

The roles of approval meeting participants are quite distinct from each other. The forum and the review teams present the evolution plan to the approval team. The approval team, meanwhile, listens to the presentations and tries to understand the plan, asking as many questions as possible. It then either adjourns to deliberate on approval of the plan or provides direction on adjustments that must be made before approval can be given.

Initial project activation. The approval team's final task in this step is to review the forum's recommended project sequence and determine whether the resources are available to support these projects. (In general, approval teams okay the priority projects but limit the number of proposed projects to be activated initially.) It is a good idea to start out by executing only priority projects in a conservative, focused manner. After these initial projects have met with some success and resource constraints have become better understood, other projects can be activated. (See explanation of Step 11.)

What have we achieved so far? This extensive but essential planning process has accomplished several things:

- It has introduced a strong sense of empowerment and involvement among employees at all levels.
- It has shifted the authority for planning to lower levels in the organization. This sets the scene for even deeper delegation when project teams are activated.

- It has changed the function of management from direction imposing to approval giving, thus strengthening the sense of group ownership over the evolution plan.
- It has provided a vehicle, by means of the structured prioritization process, for focused and orderly change.
- It has produced a strategic plan to which all company functions and levels contributed.
- It has defined a plan for continuous improvement and change that will be relevant for up to five years.
- It has created an environment of personal investment in the evolution plan. About 80 percent of the plan could be developed by managers acting alone. Having all employees "buy-in" to the plan, however, makes implementation much easier. Furthermore, if a white elephant project appears in the evolution plan, which is unusual, the approval team can quietly choose not to activate it, without bruising feelings.

In short, the planning process generates a great deal of satisfaction, excitement, and mutual commitment throughout the organization. The typical sentiment of senior managers after completing Step 6 is: We never realized how smart and knowledgeable our people are! The plan is much better than it would be if we had generated it ourselves.

On the other side, their employees say: We never thought senior management would go along with our plan. They usually don't even listen to us, let alone agree to a plan that we developed.

Obviously the "them versus us" attitude has been replaced by an environment of mutual respect, trust, and commitment. Properly managed, this "buzz" can be sustained throughout the CTM evolution. It will be short-lived, however, if the rest of the implementation steps are forgotten.

Step 7: Communicate Evolution Plan

Once the management approval team has approved the evolution plan, it must make the plan known to everyone in the organization. Each person should receive a hard copy of the plan or have access to one.

Then management should call an open meeting to present the plan's salient features and formally post the new mission statement. Strong representation by management should be apparent at this meeting. In addition, the involvement of all levels in creating the plan should be emphasized (see Figure 8-17).

Impact of plan on employee commitment. At the open meeting, the usual cry from the ranks is, *When can I get involved?* Most people want to contribute and seek involvement, especially if the CTM education program has been timed to take place just before the plan is published. The response, in fact, can be overwhelming to a project leader. The next step gives them a means of handling the demand for involvement effectively and fairly.

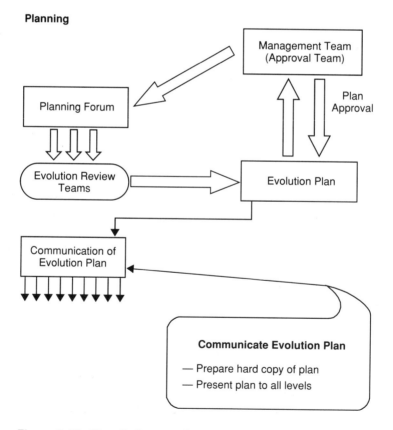

Figure 8-17. Step 7: Communicate Evolution Plan

The planning stage is now complete.

STAGE 3B: EXECUTION PHASE

The execution phase of CTM implementation comprises Steps 8 and 9 of the 12-step implementation process (see Figure 8-18). To support the execution phase, specific project leadership, teambuilding, and problem-solving education and training will be necessary so that those involved in the projects can work on planning and executing the change effectively. Also, specific CTM improvement training such as changeover reduction, pull system development, and process simplification analysis may also be appropriate to fuel the team's activities.

Recall that the review teams are formed (Step 2) to expose and document the opportunities for cycle time reduction in their "area of focus." The forum then integrates the various review teams' lists of opportunities and projects into the evolution plan for submission back to the approval team. After the evolution plan is approved (Step 6), the forum and review teams are disbanded. As part of Steps 8 and 9, project teams are activated on an ongoing basis to implement the various opportunities outlined in the evolution plan.

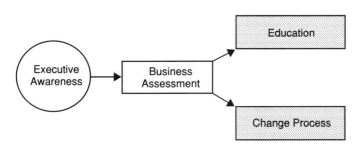

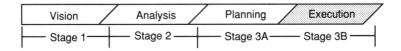

Figure 8-18. Stage 3B of CTM Implementation (Execution Phase)

Step 8: Program Kickoff

The program leaders chosen at Step 6 now hold a short resource planning meeting to discuss program kickoff (see Figure 8-19). If there are individuals involved in several projects simultaneously the program leaders may have to set priorities.

During this resource planning meeting the program leaders review the global schedules for all projects in the program. They also agree on meeting schedules and support needed from outside services.

Remember that the program leader should also be a member of the approval team. This person plays an important role in the execution phase by providing each team with both coordination and support. He or she serves as a coach to the teams and, as a member of the approval team, ensures that there is a link between them and the approval team at all times.

As the evolution plan progresses and more projects are activated, this program review may be repeated if the program leader believes it necessary. Where considerable interaction exists between projects within the program, the program leader may decide to hold a regular review to assist the project leaders in managing these interactions. Examples of such interactive projects are those involving plant (or office) layout, where common resources such as facility engineering and support groups need to be allocated according to priority.

A word of caution is needed, however: these reviews should *not* replace the monthly evolution plan review (described in Step 11) and should certainly not overstep the mandate given by the approval team.

Also, the program leader has the responsibility to ensure that the project leaders and their teams stay within their scopes and mandates and that the CTM implementation process is adhered to or at least not contravened.

The CTM structure is designed as a support system allowing everyone in the organization an opportunity to experience the new approach to managing change. Trust is earned as a product of the process, and the only prerequisite is to participate.

This process can work only with the commitment and support of management. Employees must feel comfortable with voicing

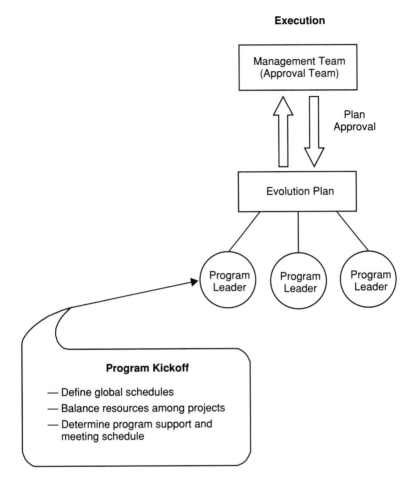

Figure 8-19. Step 8: Program Kickoff

their views and ideas. In fact, the process requires nothing less than realignment of the beliefs that people hold about their roles in the organization and thus of their personal aspirations.

Step 9: Project Kickoff

After the approval team has activated a project and the program leaders have performed a program kickoff, the project leader calls a project kickoff meeting. This will be the first formal project meeting. At this time leadership of the project is ratified. (Sometimes a natural leader is allowed to emerge, in which case the program leader calls the first meetings until project leadership is clear.) It is not unusual for the program leader to attend the first meeting and assist with the briefing on the scope and mandate of the project.

Purpose of meeting. The project kickoff meeting has several purposes:

1. to define the scope and mandate of the project
2. to define project membership
3. to define project leadership

The project team reviews, documents, and agrees on the project scope and mandate. Under the leadership of the project leader, and with the support of the project team members, feasibility studies must be developed to achieve the scope and mandate of the detailed series of project activities (see Figure 8-20).

Team meetings. After the initial project kickoff meeting, the project leaders call project meetings as needed, to develop the plans and later control the project's progress. To be effective leaders, they must have facilitation and problem-solving skills as well as be educated in the CTM concepts and tools.

Project leaders can come from any part of the organization but are usually individuals who will inherit the outcome of the project.

Team members are individuals who

- come from any part and level of the organization that will be affected by the change
- can help in planning or executing the change

Their role is to work with the project leaders on the active projects identified in the evolution plan.

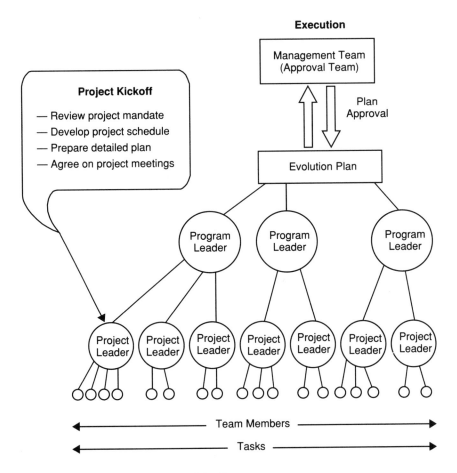

Figure 8-20. Step 9: Project Kickoff

Step 10: Management Approval Meeting

This step is essential to maintain the control of a project in keeping with the wishes of the approval team.

Preparing for the management approval meeting. The first step in preparing for the approval meeting is to get the project leader

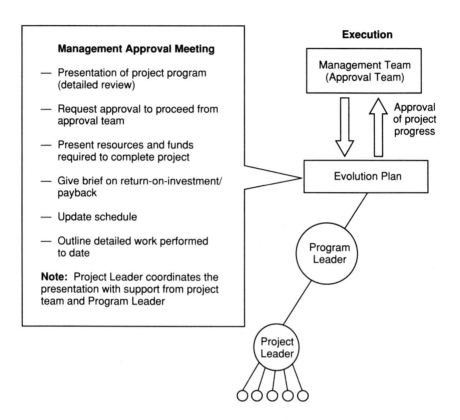

Figure 8-21. Step 10: Management Approval Meeting

(through the program leader) to put the project on the agenda of the approval team meeting. At this point the program leaders coach the project leaders in preparing their presentations to ensure that the correct information and level of detail are included (see Figure 8-21).

Thus the program leaders act as inside lobbyists on the approval team for each project within their specific program. At a minimum, they should provide moral support but may also coach project leaders and team members on presenting the project status and report. They also work with the CTM coordinator to ensure that the approval meetings take place and that all the essential approval team members attend. By gauging the success rate of the project being submitted for approval, program leaders also serve as a check prior to the approval team meeting.

Project leaders should invite their project team members to the approval meeting. The presentation — although coordinated by the project team leader — may also be presented by others on the team. In fact, the more members of the team that get involved in making presentations, the greater is the growth of the team spirit and commitment to the project.

Each project team will be asked to provide the approval team with the data that pertains to their project. To ensure an orderly process, the approval team will authorize only one phase at a time. When one phase is complete, the project leader goes back to the approval team to get the next one authorized.

CTM project implementation process. Once a project is kicked off and activated, the project leaders must follow the CTM project implementation process (see Figure 8-22). This defines the tactical control of the evolution plan. The preparation and approval of the evolution plan through Step 7 completes the strategic planning phase. From that point, the changes outlined in the plan are implemented at a more tactical project level.

CTM project status control system. The approval team assigns a status to each project at various points throughout its life. This status system enables the approval team to control all project activities and processes. The *project status* may be

- active (project team can proceed to the next phase)
- inactive (project should not be started but may be active at some future date)
- completed (project is finished except for follow-up phase)
- on hold (project has been started but must be delayed for some reason)
- cancelled (project will not contribute to the evolution plan and therefore should be stopped)

A project may be defined at the time that the evolution plan is prepared and remain inactive for some time. Then when resources become available or the time is determined to be appropriate the project is declared "active" and a kickoff meeting is held.

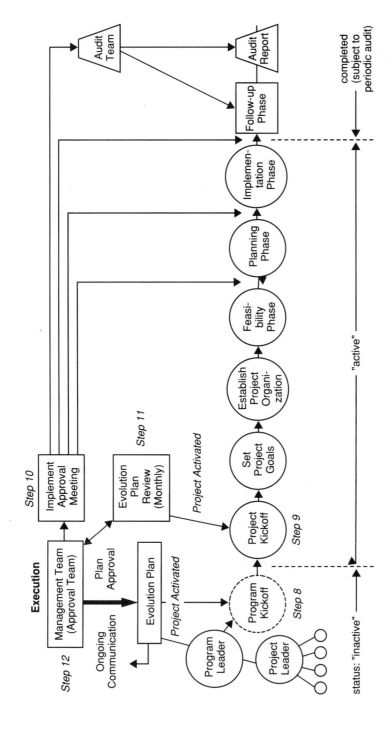

Figure 8-22. CTM Project Implementation Process

At any time the approval team (and only the approval team) may change the status of a project, depending on the information received at the approval meetings.

Project phases. After kickoff, project leaders must meet with team members to map out definitive phases in the project's life cycle. To ensure an orderly process, the approval team authorizes only one phase at a time. When one phase is complete the team makes a plan for the next phase, which the project leader and program leader then take to the approval team for authorization.

Each project has four phases (see Figure 8-22):

1. In the *feasibility phase* the project team (perhaps with the help of the program leader) puts together a report that proves the project can be accomplished and provides an estimate of base resources required and a schedule outlining the phases and expected completion dates of each. (It is important as part of the earlier project approval meeting that a clear project mandate and scope be defined. This will ensure that a clear goal is set at the project team level.)
2. In the *planning phase* team members expand the feasibility report into a more detailed written implementation plan. On some projects this will include requests and justification for funds to implement the project.
3. In the *implementation phase* the team puts the implementation plan into action.
4. During the *follow-up phase* an audit team composed of those affected by the change and members of the original project team ensure that the payback from the project has been obtained. They audit the actual outcome of the project against the planned outcome and prepare a report that is fed back to the Step 10 approval meeting. In some cases the program leaders assume the responsibility for presenting this report to the approval team.

Audit report. The audit report serves two purposes. It provides an opportunity to (1) recognize success and (2) reactivate the project if original expectations have not been achieved. Our experience is that few projects have to be reactivated; most project teams either meet or exceed the goals set out in the original project scope and mandate.

Once people take responsibility for improvement on a continuous basis — the real target of CTM — improvement goals are usually achieved.

The approval team should maintain a posture of mild surprise for successes and consistent support for below-target results. The audit is usually an opportunity to tout one's successes. One organization on the CTM fast track plans a ceremony involving all project teams once the project is completed.

Final presentations to the president and the board of directors occur in what has been described as a "real party atmosphere."

Step 11: Monthly Evolution Plan Review

Once a month, the approval team meets to reflect on the progress being made on the CTM evolution plan and to take action on any issues that require management decisions. These issues could be organizational or they could involve resource allocation. The team should also reflect on its own performance and on how it is being perceived by the rest of the organization.

The monthly review meeting has several objectives (see Figure 8-23):

- to confirm the scope and mandate of each project
- to reinforce support for project progress to date
- to realign resources across the evolution plan
- to deliberate the status changes for projects
- to identify and add new projects to the evolution plan
- to review overall progress of the evolution plan

The meeting consists of two separate sessions. First, the project leader holds a briefing session on the project team's progress to date. This is *not* an approval team meeting; its purpose is to review the project. Second, a general review of the evolution plan is held. Any change in status of existing projects or identification of new projects for the evolution plan should be discussed at this meeting.

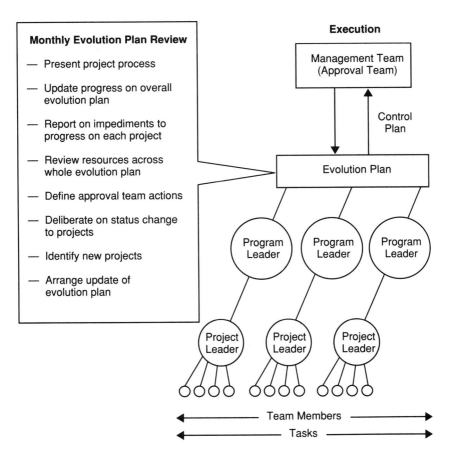

Figure 8-23. Monthly Evolution Plan Review

In most organizations operating the CTM process this is a full-day affair, with the CTM projects being reviewed in sequence and each team presenting its progress to date. Most organizations can cycle a project team through the review in 10 minutes, a time frame that allows all team members to show their support for each other and commitment to the project. The review gives teams recognition and inspires them to continue their efforts.

After reviewing all CTM projects, the approval team focuses on overall progress and project status, deciding whether to make any project status changes or take any other actions.

In the early meetings the approval team is usually uncomfortable making decisions in public. However, as members become more familiar with the CTM process and build trust in each other, their discomfort disappears. Approval teams start to encourage other parts of the organization to witness the decision process. This simple action builds understanding and commitment to the decisions across the organization. One approval team actually invites employees who can spare the time to sit through the whole meeting.

Public access of this sort continually reinforces the evolution plan and opens a direct line into that best of communication systems, the grapevine.

Step 12: Quarterly Communication Sessions

The essential ingredient for a successful evolution to CTM is the maintenance of communication links between all employees. Formal communication meetings should be scheduled at least every three months and should include strong participation by the approval team members.

The central aims of this step are to provide a global, well-balanced outline of the evolution plan's progress and to note what projects are being worked on and where the resources and effort are being concentrated. Various media should be used:

- A display board should be mounted in *at least* one place in the company showing the current status of project approvals and performance to date against the plan.
- Company newsletters should be circulated.
- A permanent CTM war room where more detailed information can be posted or stored should be created. This room should be where most of the project team meetings take place. The CTM coordinator should be responsible for both the room and the information displayed in it.
- A scale model of the layout of the physical process of the business can be used to explain, reinforce, and gain support if physical changes to the manufacturing or office areas are planned.

The important thing to remember is that to ensure strong commitment from all levels of the organization and thus a smooth transition to CTM, everyone who will be affected by the changes must either be made part of the planning process or continually informed on the changes being implemented.

STAGE 4: THE COMPETITIVE EDGE/ CONTINUOUS IMPROVEMENT

With the completion of the 12 CTM implementation steps, Stage 3 of the implementation process is finished and a mechanism for continuous improvement and change in the organization is in place (see Figure 8-24). The approval team now has the means to

- reinforce and support employee inspired change
- communicate the decisions necessary to keep the process moving
- maintain the concept of teamwork and participative management

In most cases, the continuous improvement process equips the organization to maintain a competitive edge through the 1990s and beyond.

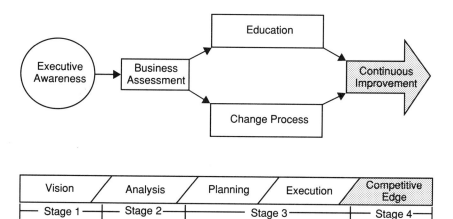

Figure 8-24. Stage 4 of CTM Implementation

As we pointed out in Chapter 5, there is a down side to the process — not everyone will be able to survive the culture change. However, the CTM 12-step implementation process ensures most individuals will have both time and practice to achieve a fit with this new culture.

9

Business Strategies for the 1990s and Beyond

OVERVIEW

As we stated in the Introduction, success for most businesses in the future will require the integration of the five cycle time loops.

The objective to this point has been to demonstrate how to reduce cycle time in the make/ship loop. The purpose of this chapter is to show how the other loops get drawn into the cycle-time reduction effort. For example, as teams focus on the impediments and nonessential activities in the make/ship loop, they discover more impediments and waste in the supply and distribution loops. Similarly, as they integrate these loops, pressure mounts to integrate the new product introduction (NPI) and strategic planning loops with the other three loops (see Figure 9-1).

As stated earlier, a company's total business cycle time is measured from the time a customer's need is identified to receipt of payment from that customer for the finished product. We defined the make/ship loop as the time from receipt of material, through the value-adding conversion steps, to shipment of a finished product to the distribution loop. Now let's examine how this loop becomes integrated with the other four loops.

There are three thrusts to the integration process:

- Integrating the supply, make/ship, and distribution loops
- Integrating the new product introduction loop
- Integrating the strategic planning loop

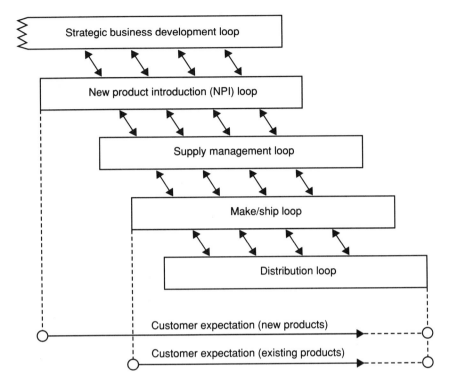

Figure 9-1. Integration of the Five Cycle Time Loops

STRATEGIC THRUST 1: INTEGRATING THE SUPPLY, MAKE/SHIP, AND DISTRIBUTION LOOPS

As the project teams review their processes in the make/ship loop they soon discover impediments that are created by supply and distribution loops. This discovery naturally leads them to look beyond the make/ship loop to the causes of those impediments.

Organizational Realignment

Some organizations encourage the integration of the supply, make/ship, and distribution loops by lumping responsibility for all procurement, manufacturing, and distribution functions under the umbrella of operations.

Whether quality assurance (QA) is included in this expanded department depends on the maturity of the organization and its commitment to quality and the regulatory controls in that industry. Many organizations will maintain the QA mandate as a separate corporate function reporting directly to the president or CEO until everyone is confident that appropriate quality performance measures are in place. Regardless of the QA role, the expanded operations organization is free to eliminate waste and drive for cycle time improvement and ultimately the integration of these three loops.

Many organizations are now following this path to integration. The closings and relocations of plants, as well as internal turmoil caused by reconsiderations of basic functions, while upsetting, are in most cases the result of companies having determined the true value-added activities in these three loops and reacting accordingly.

The integration process will raise important questions which must be answered directly. Some examples follow:

- *Why is my plant being closed and the product moved to another plant when we are productive?*

  The other plant is also productive but the other plant is more flexible and therefore does not need the support of a distribution point and can direct ship to meet real customer demand.

- *Why is customer order-entry being consolidated at the plant rather than left in the regions or sales areas?*

  Customers are demanding shorter delivery times. We want to take advantage of our short manufacturing cycle time and direct ship from the plant.

- *Why are products being moved into different plants?*

  We want to take advantage of the efficiencies of the focused factory for high-volume products and produce the low-volume specialized products in our flexible facilities.

- *Why didn't our products win the bid to supply to your company, since our price was the lowest?*

  There were other issues that were more important than price. For example:

  1. You could not or would not support a certification program to eliminate hidden costs that affect both of us.

2. We have to focus on fewer suppliers to reduce our purchasing efforts.

3. We are starting to develop partnership relationships to work together to improve overall cycle times and total quality and to reduce inventories and nonessentials that affect our mutual costs.

Direct answers to such critical issues will resound throughout the organization communicating the *total* commitment of top management to the CTM mandate, and generating a powerful momentum to complete the CTM evolution process.

STRATEGIC THRUST 2: INTEGRATING THE NEW PRODUCT INTRODUCTION LOOP

Achieving the first thrust improves the existing operations and products. What about the new generation of products? Suppose the competition is in the market with a new product before us and also has strategic thrust 1 well in hand. Who will get the future business? It is important to reduce the new product introduction (NPI) cycle time in parallel, and integrate it with the other loops as quickly as possible.

A detailed review of a modern NPI procedure is outside the scope of this book; we can say, however, that an effective procedure would include the principles contained in this chapter and serve as a framework for any company undertaking NPI cycle time reduction.

The traditional NPI approach assumed that responsibility for new products rested firmly with research and development, sometimes called design or product engineering.

In the same era that hosted that approach, marketing was perceived as fickle or unable to reach decisions. It either was forced to respond to short-term sales opportunities on a hit-or-miss basis or, if it identified a larger opportunity, had trouble developing an accurate specification for the new product for R&D. The process was complicated by the lengthy time required to get a commitment of funds from senior management. The result was a long cycle time for development and closure on a new-product strategy. The changes in product specifications generate faulty research that delays starts on new product developments and probably results in too much new product development in progress.

The final player in the traditional NPI scenario is operations. It feels misused by the other two factions and is therefore disinclined to participate in the new product development process.

In most corporations new product introduction has bordered on a bad joke with all participants emotionally enveloped in the activity. No amount of management involvement or policy can completely calm the storm. During the early 1980s, NPI cycle times actually increased in some organizations because of the added checks and balances imposed by management policies and the inevitable erosion of trust between marketing, R&D, and operations. Communication between these departments became overformal and decidedly political and protective. The following sentiments prevailed:

- Marketing doesn't know what it wants.
- R&D gives us products that don't work.
- R&D gives us products we can't make.
- Operations doesn't want to help us with new products.
- I'm fed up with promising the customer a new product — it never happens.

The eventual outcome in most large companies is a heavy proceduralized and bureaucratized NPI process with protracted cycle times that leave the companies unresponsive to the customer. They either do not have the product available, or conversely, they rush a flawed product to market and thus create an unhappy customer later.

Some corporations worked through this dilemma and thus avoided what might have been a cultural nightmare. The newer industries such as electronics, computers, and high-tech commodities found it easier to switch cultures and break down the departmental walls of the past because they had one or more of the following attributes:

- No baggage from the past to contend with
- Beginning as small outfits in which it was not unusual to design a product one day, make it the next, and sell it the day after
- Competition within the industry for new products and thus a strong anticulture to nonessential internal competition

In the CTM NPI approach, integration of the loops is tied to cycle time improvement in the NPI loop. Indeed, one drives the other.

Teams are essential to this approach, just as they are to the launching of high-quality new products in minimum cycle time. When working for the space program in the early 1970s one team was told the following by one of the senior managers: "I'm going to lock you all in one room and push pizza under the door until you have the solution. The quicker you get a solution the better, for there is only one bag of gold — a communication satellite in orbit." This manager's role in the room was to make the coffee and cut the pizza. The product was the solution; the "product team" was the people in that room.

This is a simple example of the team approach. But how do we lock an entire organization in one room, give it one goal, and get it to work collectively toward that goal with minimal confrontation and supervision?

Product Teams

The purpose of the product team is to meld R&D, marketing, operations and any other specialists that are required. This team structure is built along both organizational and cultural lines. To be successful, project teams require a set of common guidelines and a commitment by senior management to provide resources and support. While certain skills come into play more than others at various points during the product life cycle, the NPI process cannot work if it is perceived to be the responsibility of one department. Once formed, a product team must not only launch new products but also support and sustain existing products within its mandate.

The NPI process, using the product team approach, is not a department, not an individual, not a single function, and not a constraint. It is a *framework*. When this mentality is embedded successfully within the culture then the product team approach can flourish.

Such an environment for new products not only promotes a shortened cycle time to define, develop, and launch the product, but also provides a mechanism to integrate tools and concepts that were ignored under the old system. Examples of these now usable tools are design for manufacturability (DFM), group technology, design/process sigma analysis, early product modeling, and design simulation. The interdepartmental gate can be opened to allow the sharing of cross-functional data with computerized tools such as computer-aided engineering (CAE) and computer-aided process planning (CAPP). The sharing of new designs and manufacturing technologies and the integration of these into new product strategies is best accomplished in the team environment.

When the NPI cycle times are reduced, learning cycles for new generations of products will be enhanced. A stable product team provides a platform on which all team members can learn from each product generation and reapply this learning to the next generation. Note that *shorter NPI cycle times mean more learning cycles and hence a higher learning rate and faster improvements from one product generation to another.*

The product team should focus on improving cycle times, enhancing quality, and reducing total product cost for each new generation of product. Some corporations have made each product a profit center and encourage healthy interteam rivalry. In the new culture, involvement with a new product is a positive experience rather than a negative one. In the old culture, new products were given cold-sounding code numbers like XX02, BA4, and 6002. The new culture gives its products real names even before they are born — Spitfire, Jupiter, Zoom, Saturn, Alpha are some of the ones we've encountered. In fact, even after these products receive their final code numbers and official market names, the teams still refer to them affectionately by their old names. Such names build a sense of ownership over the product throughout its life cycle.

Product Team Leadership

Usually a core team of senior design, marketing, and operations people head up the product team and delegate specific projects to junior team members. How this is done and how this matrix organization works varies from organization to organization. Some have formal product management organizations in which the team approach is achieved by a management organization, while others have an informal product team organization in which a core team of managers coordinate the team's activities. While it is essential to have one person coordinate the product team's activities, responsibility for the activities themselves should be evenly distributed. Thus the marketing representative will carry the baton through the product definition phase; R&D or design engineering will carry it through the development phase; operations will stand by to pull the product through the various manufacturing checkpoints and pass it into the customer's hands.

Early involvement in the product team by all functions builds consensus and commitment to the new product and minimizes the chances that conflicting perceptions of the product will emerge.

We have seen product teams involve suppliers and even customers early in the NPI process, with great benefits for each group. A product team is not a committee that manages consensus. Each team member must still have the authority and respect of all other team members to make judgments and final decisions in his or her area of responsibility. The objective is to concur that the best job is being done to meet the product team objectives, given the information, ideas, and issues that they have shared. This is a fine line to walk. A procedural framework and strong management leadership are required to maintain the internal balance of power and mutual respect.

Design for Manufacturability

We mentioned earlier that various tools and concepts could be more readily applied to the NPI process once a team approach was adapted. The most powerful of these is design for manufacturability (DFM). This acronym covers a broad spectrum of design methodologies. Included are design for

- assembly
- fabrication
- supply
- testing
- quality
- user-friendliness
- disassembly
- inspection
- field service
- reliability
- procurement
- processing

- distribution
- group technology
- functionality
- cost-effectiveness
- price negotiations
- regulations acceptance
- environment and conservation
- obsolescence
- compatibility
- aesthetics
- zero-changeovers
- zero-fixturing

To be successful, you must embrace all of the facets and skills connected with the above list. DFM relies upon the product team culture that underpins the NPI philosophy.

Some of the DFM inputs to the design can be handled with design rules or specifications. Some can be embedded into design tools, such as CAE/CAD workstations using logic programmed into the computer software. Others need to be handled interactively through team discussion and even physical trials so that the various design trade-offs can be optimized.

The DFM concept has become a cultural issue where the modern engineer or design specialists must relinquish their status as prime innovators for one as collaborators willing to accept input. This adjustment can lead to culture *shock* for some engineers schooled in the "we design, you make" tradition. Marketing specialists and operations people also must be prepared to receive input from other disciplines.

DFM is based on the philosophy that problems must be solved through an interdisciplinary effort: *you can't do it alone and it can't be done without you.*

This spirit of cooperation and sharing does not come naturally in most organizations. When creating a product team structure expect to meet with frustration, confrontation, and less than optimal decisions. Reinforcing the team approach to NPI will take forceful and consistent leadership from management. It will also require a new awareness of product team essentials by all members. This awareness can be achieved through education, practice, and reinforcement of the concepts of product teams and the DFM concept.

The product team that applies DFM concepts will either achieve the NPI goals or draw within reach for them. Using this approach, many corporations have achieved benefits such as improved product cost and quality performance and, of course, reduced time to market. Some have witnessed a slight extension of product time to market, but the delay was more than offset by increases in reliability and quality.

Cycle Time Improvement

The first step in improving cycle time is to create an environment in which product teams can function. The CTM 12-step implementation process should be used to expose the opportunities for cycle time improvement and establish the proper environment for NPI product teams. The outcome of this process is the creation of the teams.

Continuous cycle time improvement starts once the product team is formed. The same CTM principles and tools used to improve the other cycle time loops apply to this loop also. NPI is a business process with its own forms of value- and non–value-added activities. The impediments will be different, but the means are the same: elimination of the cause of impediments leads to removal of the impediments and simplification of the process.

A few examples of cycle time improvements follow:

- The checking of drawings as a separate function is an impediment. The team who created the drawing and the process operators who first use them at the prototype stage should check them.
- A policy dictating multiple sign-offs of drawings is an impediment. The team that creates the drawing should take responsibility for it.

- A practice of making multiple physical models of a product through development and launch is an impediment. Identify why some models are really needed, define ways of combining the development and launch process requirements for these models, and reduce the number of model types to perhaps two — a development model and a production model. That number, although ideal, is difficult to achieve. The benefit, however, is shorter cycle time without detriment to product cost, quality, or functional objectives.

Definition of a New Product

What is a new product? Many arguments have taken place over the distinction between a new product and a slight modification to an existing product. Our own view is that it is a new product if there are

- any changes to the fit/form/function
- any perceived change to fit/form/function by customers
- any changes to design and manufacturing processes, methods, or technology that could contribute to fit/form/function
- new market requirements that effect any change in the product offering (such as new labels for export)

The role of the product team is to determine how much of the new product introduction process must be activated for a given product: What risks do we run if we just short-circuit the process and slap on a new label in production? Should we prototype it and get input to the new label? These are examples of the questions that might be asked.

This dilemma illustrates why the NPI process should be a framework that enables product teams to manage the risks of product change or introduction, and why it should emphasize a control methodology without overdue bureaucratic constraints.

In the end, success in installing the NPI process will not be obtained from a book or a consultant. It will be the result of hard experience in adapting the concepts of CTM and applying the 12-step implementation process.

STRATEGIC THRUST 3: INTEGRATING THE STRATEGIC PLANNING LOOP

Neither a best-in-class supplier/make-ship/distribution capability nor a world-class NPI capability assures you of success. To exploit the benefits provided by integration of the other four loops, you must also have a low cycle time strategic planning loop. Integrating this loop is essential to maintaining and even accelerating the corporate success achieved to date, for it is the strategic plan that outlines whether and how the company will

- grow or shrink
- acquire or divest
- integrate or separate
- develop or liquidate

As stated in the Introduction, the problems in this loop have to do with size, politics, economics, and legal and financial inertia, all of which add time. The big companies have two problems to overcome: First, most businesses lack the methodology and process necessary to shorten the cycle time in this loop. Second, reducing total business cycle time is perceived at all levels as risky, disruptive, emotionally wearing, and rarely put into practice. As a result, reductions in the cycle time of this loop become more compelling, however, organizations must gain confidence in the benefits of these changes.

As some of the old *Fortune* 500 companies are discovering, the 1990s markets will belong to those who eliminate the red-tape, can make decisions and execute them in minimal cycle time.

The strategic business development loop is the prime mover for total business improvement. Fancy words such as synergy and market share and capital contributions are often used, but it is very rare that the overall business cycle time is labeled, either as an area for improvement or a parameter to be coordinated through the strategic planning process.

A short strategic planning loop ensures that all five loops will be integrated and embeds continuous cycle time reduction into the corporate culture. It also enables senior managers of large companies to be entrepreneurial and to increase company profits, because they will be able to seize market opportunities faster, with less risk and smaller investment.

About the Authors

Patrick Northey

Patrick Northey is a chartered accountant with long and varied experience as a consultant and educator. He is President of Interaction Limited, a firm focusing on change management and productivity improvement, and was a founding partner of Cycle Time Management, Inc. He has given seminars and worked with businesses in Canada and the United States. Formerly he was a professor in the School of Business at Ryerson Polytechnical Institute and taught at Ryerson's Center for Advanced Technology Education in Toronto.

Nigel C. Southway

Nigel Southway has spent most of his business career as a consultant to major manufacturing companies. In 1985, he joined Motorola Corporation to develop and implement an evolution plan for Canadian operations, based on the concept of total business cycle time. This experience led him to his current consulting position at Cycle Time Management, Inc., in Toronto. Through Cycle Time Management, Mr. Southway has consulted to numerous firms in Canada and the United States.

Index

OTHER BOOKS FROM PRODUCTIVITY PRESS

Productivity Press publishes and distributes materials on continuous improvement in productivity, quality, and the creative involvement of all employees. Many of our products are direct source materials from Japan that have been translated into English for the first time and are available exclusively from Productivity. Supplemental products and services include membership groups, conferences, seminars, in-house training and consulting, audio-visual training programs, and industrial study missions. Call toll-free 1-800-394-6868 for our free catalog.

A New American TQM
Four Practical Revolutions in Management

Shoji Shiba, Alan Graham, and David Walden

For TQM to succeed in America, you need to create an American-style "learning organization" with the full commitment and understanding of senior managers and executives. Written expressly for this audience, A New American TQM offers a comprehensive and detailed explanation of TQM and how to implement it, based on courses taught at MIT's Sloan School of Management and the Center for Quality Management, a consortium of American hi-tech companies. Full of case studies and amply illustrated, the book examines major quality tools and how they are being used by the most progressive American companies today.
ISBN 1-56327-032-3 / 500 pages / $49.95 / Order NATQM-B127

Vision Management
Translating Strategy into Action

SANNO Management Development Research Center (ed.)

For over ten years, managers of Japan's top companies have gathered at SANNO University to brainstorm about innovative corporate management methods. This book is based on the proven methodology that evolved from their ideas. It describes how the intangible aspects of vision-based strategy can be integrated into a concrete implementation model and clarifies the relationship among vision, strategy, objectives, goals, and day-to-day activities.
ISBN 0-915299-80-1 / 272 pages / $29.95 / Order VISM-B127

Productivity Press, Inc., Dept. BK, P.O. Box 3007, Cambridge, MA 02140 1-800-274-9911

Hoshin Kanri
Policy Deployment for Successful TQM
Yoji Akao (ed.)

Hoshin kanri, the Japanese term for policy deployment, is an approach to strategic planning and quality improvement that has become a pillar of Total Quality Management (TQM) for a growing number of U.S. firms. This book is a compilation of examples of policy deployment that demonstrates how company vision is converted into individual responsibility. It includes practical guidelines, 150 charts and diagrams, and five case studies that illustrate the procedures of hoshin kanri. The six steps to advanced process planning are reviewed and include a five-year vision, one-year plan, deployment to departments, execution, monthly audit, and annual audit.

ISBN 0-915299-57-7 / 256 pages / $65.00 / Order HOSHIN-B127

Measuring, Managing, and Maximizing Performance
Will Kaydos

You do not need to be an exceptionally skilled technician or inspirational leader to improve your company's quality and productivity. In non-technical, jargon-free, practical terms this book details the entire process of improving performance, from why and how the improvement process work to what must be done to begin and to sustain continuous improvement of performance. Special emphasis is given to the role that performance measurement plays in identifying problems and opportunities.

ISBN 0-915299-98-4 / 304 pages / $39.95 Order MMMP-B127

Performance Measurement for World Class Manufacturing
A Model for American Companies
Brian H. Maskell

If your company is adopting world class manufacturing techniques, you'll need new methods of performance measurement to control production variables. In practical terms, this book describes the new methods of performance measurement and how they are used in a changing environment. For manufacturing managers as well as cost accountants, it provides a theoretical foundation of these innovative methods supported by extensive practical examples. The book specifically addresses performance measures for delivery, process time, production flexibility, quality, and finance.

ISBN 0-915299-99-2 / 448 pages / $55.00 / Order PERFM-B127

Productivity Press, Inc., Dept. BK, P.O. Box 3007, Cambridge, MA 02140 1-800-274-9911

20 Keys to Workplace Improvement

Iwao Kobayashi

This easy-to-read introduction to the "20 keys" system presents an integrated approach to assessing and improving your company's competitive level. The book focuses on systematic improvement through five levels of achievement in such primary areas as industrial housekeeping, small group activities, quick changeover techniques, equipment maintenance, and computerization. A scoring guide is included, along with information to help plan a strategy for your company's world class improvement effort.
ISBN 0-915299-61-5 / 264 pages / $39.95 / Order 20KEYS-B227

Managerial Engineering
Techniques for Improving Quality and Productivity in the Workplace

Ryuji Fukuda

A proven path to managerial success, based on reliable methods developed by one of Japan's leading productivity experts and winner of the coveted Deming Prize for quality. Dr. W. Edwards Deming, world-famous consultant on quality, says that the book "provides an excellent and clear description of the devotion and methods of Japanese management to continual improvement of quality." (Training programs on CEDAC, the award-winning system outlined in this book, are also available from Productivity.)
ISBN 0-915299-09-7 / 208 pages / $44.95 / Order ME-B127

Quality Function Deployment
Integrating Customer Requirements into Product Design

Yoji Akao (ed.)

Written by the creator of QFD, this book provides direct source material on one of the essential tools for world class manufacturing. More and more companies are using QFD to identify customer requirements, translate them into quantified quality characteristics, and then build them into their products and services. This casebook introduces the concept of quality deployment as it has been applied in a variety of industries in Japan.
ISBN 0-915299-41-0 / 387 pages / $85.00 / Order QFD-B127

Productivity Press, Inc., Dept. BK, P.O. Box 3007, Cambridge, MA 02140 1-800-274-9911

Concurrent Engineering
Shortening Lead Times, Raising Quality, and Lowering Costs

John R. Hartley

By simultaneously taking into account the concerns of design, production, purchasing, finance, and marketing from the very first stages of product planning, concurrent engineering makes doing it right the first time the rule instead of the exception. An introductory handbook, this text gives managers 16 clear guidelines for achieving concurrent engineering and provides abundant case studies of Japanese, U.S., and European successes.
ISBN 1-56327-006-4 / 330 pages / $60.00 / Order CONC-B127

Function Analysis
Systematic Improvement of Quality and Performance

Kaneo Akiyama

Function Analysis is a systematic technique for isolating and analyzing various functions in order to better design and improve products. This book gives you a solid understanding of Function Analysis as a tool for system innovation and improvement; it helps you design your products and systems for improved manufacturability and quality. It describes how Function Analysis can be used in the office as well as on the shop floor.
ISBN 0-915299-81-X / 269 pages / $60.00 / Order FA-B127

TO ORDER: Phone or fax Productivity Press, Dept. BK, phone 1-800-394-6868, fax 1-800-394-6286, and charge to your credit card (American Express, Visa, MasterCard accepted).

U.S. ORDERS: Add $5 shipping for first book, $2 each additional for UPS surface delivery. Add $5 for each AV program containing 1 or 2 tapes; add $12 for each AV program containing 3 ore more tapes. CT residents add 6% and MA residents add 5% for sales tax. We offer attractive quantity discounts for bulk purchases of individual titles; call for more information.

INTERNATIONAL ORDERS: Write, phone, or fax for quote and indicate shipping method desired. Prepayment in U.S. dollars must accompany your order (checks must be drawn on U.S. banks).
When quote is returned with payment, your order will be shipped promptly by the method requested.

NOTE: Price are in U.S. dollars and are subject to change without notice. Please ascertain current price before ordering any products listed here.

Productivity Press, Inc., Dept. BK, P.O. Box 3007, Cambridge, MA 02140 1-800-274-9911